CONTEMPORARY ISSUES IN YOUTH SPORTS

CONTEMPORARY ISSUES IN YOUTH SPORTS

LOIS J. BARON

Nova Science Publishers, Inc.
New York

For permission to use material from this book please contact us:
Telephone 631-231-7269; Fax 631-231-8175
Web Site: http://www.novapublishers.com

NOTICE TO THE READER

The Publisher has taken reasonable care in the preparation of this book, but makes no expressed or implied warranty of any kind and assumes no responsibility for any errors or omissions. No liability is assumed for incidental or consequential damages in connection with or arising out of information contained in this book. The Publisher shall not be liable for any special, consequential, or exemplary damages resulting, in whole or in part, from the readers' use of, or reliance upon, this material.

Independent verification should be sought for any data, advice or recommendations contained in this book. In addition, no responsibility is assumed by the publisher for any injury and/or damage to persons or property arising from any methods, products, instructions, ideas or otherwise contained in this publication.

This publication is designed to provide accurate and authoritative information with regard to the subject matter covered herein. It is sold with the clear understanding that the Publisher is not engaged in rendering legal or any other professional services. If legal or any other expert assistance is required, the services of a competent person should be sought. FROM A DECLARATION OF PARTICIPANTS JOINTLY ADOPTED BY A COMMITTEE OF THE AMERICAN BAR ASSOCIATION AND A COMMITTEE OF PUBLISHERS.

LIBRARY OF CONGRESS CATALOGING-IN-PUBLICATION DATA

Baron, Lois J.
Contemporary issues in youth sports / Lois J. Baron.
    p. cm.
ISBN-13: 978-1-60021-538-4 (hardcover)
ISBN-10: 1-60021-538-6 (hardcover)
1. Sports for children. 2. Parent and child. 3. Sports for children--Social aspects. 4. Sports for children--Psychological aspects. I. Title.
GV709.2.B37   2006
796.083--dc22   2006038058

Published by Nova Science Publishers, Inc. ✦ New York

DEDICATION

I dedicate this book to the memory of my parents Brenda Joseph-Baron and Henry A. Baron. I thank them for helping me discover the world of sport and for encouraging me to pursue a diversity of sports that infinitely has enriched my life.

CONTENTS

PREFACE

Working on this book has indeed been a "labor of love". Immersing myself in theory and research related to issues in youth sport has provided me with the opportunity to share with readers the positive features of, concerns about, and controversies that surround the five topics that I have chosen to explore for this publication. Writing this book also has been a stimulating learning experience. I particularly am delighted that I have uncovered both potentially important questions to be tackled by researchers as well as topics related to youth sport that parents, coaches and athletes should become aware of and possibly address.

I have been an active participant in sport throughout my life. Growing up in Montreal in the fifties and sixties did not provide me with the wealth of opportunities that children today have in organized sport. My friends and I played all kinds of sport in our backyards or on neighboring streets. We had fun! Adults did not organize our activities, nor did we have uniforms. However, we looked forward to going outside to play after a long winter. That is what sport was to me—sport as play, sport as a game. Win or lose, we all remained friends, and happily went home looking forward to the next day when we could don our football helmets (in my case, my brother's!), or grab our baseball mitt and bat once again.

Who has had the better youth sport experience is a moot point. However, with the ever-growing number of youth participating in sport, organized or otherwise, important issues more recently have surfaced related to the involvement of parents, issues of fair play, child abuse, life skill development through sport and the commercialization of sport. Naturally, both developmental and gender issues occupy a place in any discussion revolving around children. As a developmental psychologist, I have attempted to review each issue with the goal of integrating both factors where appropriate.

Why have I chosen to cover these topics? Naturally, there are other concerns within the world of youth sport and physical activity that also need to be addressed by all stakeholders (e.g., obesity or substance abuse). However, extensive reviews related to the five topics covered in this book are generally unavailable in either the research literature or more general youth sport community. The issues of obesity and substance abuse in sport have been widely reviewed. Furthermore, in writing this book, I have attempted to balance both the research literature and practical applications.

One could not write a book about contemporary issues in youth sport without addressing the role of parents. My view is that the media has projected a very negative view of the involvement of parents in their children's sporting experiences without also examining the positive contribution that both mothers and fathers make. Needless to say, there have been several incidents reported in the media that paint a very bleak picture of parents as they threaten coaches, referees and even their own children. Unfortunately, these are the stories that make the headlines. A parent waking up at 4:00 a.m. to take their daughter to swimming practice or to an out-of-town competition is not news! The latter parents are the unsung heroes of youth sport. They play many roles as they encourage their children to participate in sport and support their child athlete whether they win or lose. Parents wear many hats (e.g., coach, fund-raiser, motivator, chauffeur, and counselor to name a few) while juggling their own careers and tending to the needs of those they support. My goal in reviewing the literature related to this topic is to demonstrate that parents can play a fundamental role in how their children perceive sport and whether the latter continue to pursue sport as a means of maintaining an active lifestyle. I also examine children's reflected appraisals of their parents' attitudes toward their participation in sport and how these reflections impact on child athletes' motivations and aspirations.

The topic of fair play in youth sport includes such issues as the development of moral character through sport and how significant others influence children's sense of sportspersonship through the motivational orientation that permeates their sport experiences. The issue of fair play in sport is a complex one that involves factors related to both the people involved in sport including parents, coaches and youth as well as the various situations that child athletes encounter through their participation in sport. In this chapter, I cover the research, and emphasize, as I do throughout the book, the importance of education and the development of self-awareness in all stakeholders regarding the elements of fair play. I call for the education of all in order to make sport an honorable venue where youth can develop and test out their moral attitudes and beliefs as they both prepare for life and attempt to fashion their world based on sound ethical principles.

As I mention at the beginning of the chapter on abuse in youth sport, it initially was not my intention to cover this area of work. However, the more I delved into the literature on this topic, the more I felt the need to share this knowledge base with readers. I immersed myself into the theoretical literature on child abuse and child protection while attempting to capture the essence of the limited yet growing body of research in what I began to view as one of the most critical concerns surrounding youth sport. In this chapter, I define the nature of child abuse, and how sport can serve as a venue for all forms of abuse to occur— neglect, sexual, physical, and emotional abuse. I describe the characteristics of perpetrators and victims and the toxic relationships that can develop. My primary goal is to heighten awareness of the qualities of both parties in an attempt to help thwart what appears to be a growing problem. I emphasize the need for primary prevention strategies where children's knowledge of and already existing participation in sport can serve as a springboard for the development of intervention programs before, not after, incidents of abuse occur. Unfortunately and quite surprisingly, there is little evidence-based intervention work in this area. My goal in writing this chapter is to educate. My hope is that both researchers and practitioners involved in youth sport will recognize, as I did, the urgency in pursuing work in this area. As with the issue of fair play, sport must be a safe and healthy environment for all youth!

The chapter on sport psychology for young athletes is one that is past due. While sport psychology has become increasingly popular, there are few inclusive reviews on how children can benefit from mental or psychological skill training. Throughout the chapter, I emphasize that psychological skill training has applications well beyond sport including life skill development that could serve children over their lifespan. I emphasize in the chapter that schools should be mandated to teach life skill development by including yearlong subject matter within the curriculum. The chapter is divided into discussions about interventions with youth sport coaches and psychological skill training for adolescents and children. Throughout the chapter, I cover theory and research the application of which could benefit students at all levels, researchers, teachers and coaches. I emphasize the use of goal setting, imagery and relaxation training, and coping for adolescents and young children. While more needs to be done in this area, I present some very encouraging research and practical applications that could serve as a catalyst for increased interest in what I consider a central area of youth sport and life.

Writing the chapter on the commercial side of sport brought me back to my original research roots—children and television. Unfortunately, social scientists have generally left this area of work untouched with the exception of those interested in the more general area of the effects of advertising on children. Yet, those in the world of marketing are at the leading edge of research into consumer behavior and marketing strategies, and are hard at work attempting to get hold of a market of young children whom they view as future consumers of sport paraphernalia. Sport and business have become intertwined at both the professional and amateur levels as athletes seek money to support their dreams while corporations put them under contract to sell products. The main goal of the chapter is to heighten readers' awareness of such marketing strategies as product endorsements, the development of brand awareness and identity, and using athletes and athletic events to sell consumer goods. My expectation is that those in contact with youth will use the information in the chapter to enlighten children about marketing schemes designed to influence and subsequently sell them products.

Finally, a principal goal in writing this book is to stimulate discussion about the above and other issues relevant to the field of youth sport. My wish is that the book will serve as vehicle for posing new questions or clarifying those that have yet to be resolved. I want those involved in research to examine the diverse methodologies used in this area of work and to expand on or create new avenues for investigation. Another objective is for coaches, parents, teachers and administrators involved in youth sport to think about the range of results discussed in this book with an eye toward incorporating the latter into practical applications that enhance the experiences of youth. Ultimately, this is the primary challenge.

ACKNOWLEDGEMENTS

I would like to thank Rosemary Razy, BSW, for her interest in and feedback on the chapter about abuse in youth sport. Her concern about issues in this area has opened up new avenues of study for me.

Chapter 1

PARENTS INVOLVEMENT IN YOUTH SPORT

The headlines in a local paper scream, "Hockey dad barred", or, "Hockey-parent outbursts persist despite efforts" (Erin, 2005). In another example of the stereotypical portrayal of a youth sport parent, a cartoon depicts two hockey parents, mother and dad, in the "out of control parent box" (Nease, January 23, 2005). The father is strangling the coach while the child sits embarrassed in the penalty box.

Hedstrom and Gould (2004) have summarized some of the more negative characteristics related to parental involvement in youth sport. These included:

- Overemphasizing winning;
- Holding unrealistic expectations;
- Coaching one's own child;
- Criticizing one's child; and
- Pampering their child too much" (p. 31).

There is no question that parents can play a very significant role, both positive and negative, in the socialization of young children particularly in youth sport where participant numbers are high. What, however, are the messages that today's parents are sending to young sport participants? Are young athletes hearing, "it's o.k. to yell at others", "it's o.k. to hit a referee or coach", or perhaps, "it's o.k. to use foul language toward others?" Are they also conveying to their children the message that one should win at all costs ("all costs" possibly meaning injurying others, Hamstra, 2002), and if you fail to come first, watch out? Or, is there a more silent "voice" portraying parents as generally supportive of their children's participation in sport and encouraging the latter to have fun, socialize and do the best they can? Another question begging a response is why some parents are so absorbed in their children's sporting lives? Are there personal voids or unfulfilled dreams in the backgrounds of these individuals such that they perceive their children's satisfying them? Finally, why has the media's focus generally been negative?

The headlines, TV programs and cartoons have painted an ugly picture of the over-involvement of parents in their children's sporting lives (e.g., "Little League parent syndrome" or "sport rage", Docheff & Conn, 2004, p. 63). However, have research results actually conformed to popular opinion? Docheff and Conn have erred in, first, assuming that little 'scientific' research has investigated this phenomenon and second, in suggesting that parental behavior is "out of control at youth sporting events" (p. 63). An ever-increasing body of research exists the goal of which has been to examine the relationship between parental support and pressure and such factors as young athletes' self-esteem, participation, motivations and personal attributions for success in sport as well as attrition and ultimately their enjoyment in both competitive and non-competitive sport.

The research on parental support of youth sport appears mixed, but the media whether film, television or newspapers (public service announcements included) have given the general impression that parents have a negative influence on their children's participation in youth sport and health behaviors. On the other hand, to its credit (and an example of constructive broadcasting), the Canadian Broadcasting Corporation screened a program entitled "The Tournament". This show satirically depicted the stereotypical 'hockey dad' applying pressure on his son and picking fights with his boss and fellow parents in an effort to promote his son's hockey skill and ability to compete. The program was blunt and evocative. On viewing it, I unfortunately had envisioned some parents cheering for the father while also hoping that many would question his extreme behavior.

Is the world of the 'hockey parent' as portrayed in the above TV program substantiated by the growing amount of research activity on the subject? Earlier research (e.g., Dunlap & Berne, Ewing & Seefeldt, Brustad, Cohn, Smoll, as cited by DeFrancesco & Johnson, 1997) generally had uncovered support for the above negative view of the sports parent. However, the 1990s saw the advent of workshops, educational programs, and websites for parents, coaches and athletes as well as a growing body of research studies designed to address the issue.

GENERAL RESEARCH FINDINGS

Due to the emphasis on the negative as related to parents and youth sport, it might surprise some to know that there is a body of some very positive findings in the research literature on parental involvement. For example, Davison (2004) has referred to a number of studies linking parental support in the forms of encouragement, joint participation, beliefs in their child's competencies and transportation to sporting events to enhanced physical activity.

In another work, Hoyle and Left (1997) appropriately emphasized the multi-faceted, complex nature of the relationship between parents and their child athletes. They examined the roles of both facilitative parental behaviors and parental pressure (e.g., unrealistic expectations, criticism, parents' reactions to a loss) with a sample of young, ranked, tennis players (ages 9 – 17). Self-reports uncovered a significant positive relationship between parental support and both children's enjoyment of tennis and the importance they placed on playing tennis. A negative link was uncovered between the players' perceptions of parental support and performance albeit this is not a consistent research finding. Objective ratings of performance, however, were positively linked which underscores the need to better define parental pressure (including looking at parent-related variables like personality, conscientiousness and goal orientation, Braddock & Petrie, 2005). Parental pressure also significantly correlated with gender -- females feeling "more of the heat". Self-esteem, however, did not serve as a mediating factor in the parental support-enjoyment relationship as had been found in other work. Finally, Hoyle and Left highlighted the need to research in greater depth the relationships among such factors as enjoyment, importance of the sport in a child's life, and the nature of supportive parental involvement. We learn through their work that these links are not as clear-cut as one might think. In fact, more recent work in this area has supported this more comprehensive view.

For example, Jambor (1999) compared the attitudes of a sample of parents who had children in youth soccer (ages 5 - 10) to those who did not (a ratio of 3:1). She sensed that understanding parental attitudes could provide insights into children's socialization as related to issues of participation and attrition in youth sport. Jambor uncovered significant differences between parents whose children participated in soccer and those whose children did not with regard to how the parents viewed the benefits of sport participation. The two parent groups held contrasting attitudes toward such factors as age appropriateness; health, recreational and physical activity benefits; and satisfaction with coaches. The parents of participating children believed that sport instills positive values. They spent more time practicing skills with their children, provided financial support for their child's participation, and attended more games and practices. On the surface, Jambor's findings seem positive. However, she did recognize the fact that research on the effects of sport parenting also must examine more closely children's own behaviors and attitudes. Isolating factors as Jambor had done was a good first step. Nevertheless, the issue of parental involvement in youth sports, as already has been emphasized in this chapter, is a multi-dimensional and complex phenomenon. There became a need to expand on work that only highlighted linear relationships between parental involvement and child-related factors.

For example, in their study, Stein, Raedeke, and Glenn (1999) discovered that young adolescents perceptions of the degree of parental involvement had more of an effect on stress and enjoyment than the level of involvement itself. In addition, holding quantity of parental involvement constant, some youth perceived the involvement as negative while others viewed it as positive. Again, a finding of this nature suggests that the relationship between parental sport involvement and such factors as children's motivations to participate, attributions for success and attitudes toward sport are not purely linear. There appears to be a zone of optimal parental involvement (so to speak) for each child. Supporting this belief, Stein, Raedeke, and Glenn revealed that children who participated in volleyball, soccer or football reacted differentially to parental involvement on measures of stress and enjoyment. Their data also uncovered curvilinear relationships between parental involvement on both of these variables. Both too little and too much perceived parental involvement had a negative impact.

If there have been reservations about parents and coaches influencing children's motivation for and enjoyment of sports, what transpires when parents coach? Can this lead to a "deadly" combination? Do parent-coaches differentially influence their child athlete? Ten per cent of the parents in Jambor's (1999) study were parent-coaches. However, unfortunately, she did not tease this out as a factor. Using Eccles' expectancy-value model that supports the view that parents influence their children's motives, Barber, Sukhi, and White (1999) did. They investigated the effects of parent-coaches' on young athletes' (ages 9-14) participation motivation and competitive state anxiety (state anxiety being anxiety related to a particular situation rather than more stable, general feelings of anxiety). Essentially, they examined whether parents who coach their own children add more pressure making the sport experience a relatively more negative one. The Participation Motivation Inventory (PMI) developed by Gill and colleagues was used to measure reasons for children's participation in sport while Martens, Vealey and Burton's Competitive State Anxiety Inventory-2 (CSAI-2) assessed cognitive anxiety (e.g., negative thoughts), somatic anxiety (i.e., bodily feelings), and self-confidence. The researchers did not uncover any negative impact when a group of parent-coached children (mixed girls and boys) were compared to those with uninvolved parents on measures of participation motivation and competitive state anxiety. Barber, Sukhi and White reported only subtle differences between parent- and non-parent-coached children's rankings of motives (e.g., parent-coached children reported wanting to improve their skills while the non-parent-coached children expressed an interest in learning new skills). These differences, albeit slight, did demonstrate variability in children's interpretations of parents' beliefs and behavior—an important variable in the parental involvement-youth sport equation. Such task-oriented responses such as "fun" and "learn new skills" were the most oft-stated factors of both groups. Barber, Sukhi and White discovered gender differences in self-reported motives with boys' being more achievement/status oriented. The researchers concluded that the boys were more socialized to achieve at sport, a common belief, while girls play. If girls play, why did female tennis players feel more pressure from their parents in Hoyt and Left's (1997) work? As girls become more active in competitive sport, will future research uncover similar results? With respect to other variables, parent-coached and non-parent-coached groups were similar on ratings of competitive state anxiety with low cognitive and somatic anxiety and higher self-confidence characteristic of both groups.   Weiss and Fretwell (2005) used semi-structured interviews with all stakeholders in boy's soccer to examine the nature of parent-coaches' influence. They concluded that the relationship was rather complex as, for example, the players reported experiencing some role confusion with regard to whether their coach interacted with them as a parent or coach. Results of their work uncovered both positive and negative consequences. The researchers called for both further work on the influence of parent-coaches and for the latter to be better informed as to how to maximize their instructional relationship with their child-athlete. All coaches would benefit from similar instruction.

Addressing the matter of self-regulation and using a more qualitative approach to data gathering, Cumming and Ewing (2002) raised the issue of children's feeling a lack of control over their sports choices and interactions if they had over-involved parents. Feelings of being controlled resulted in lack of enjoyment, low interest and possible dropout. Using the Parent Observation Instrument for Sport Events (POISE, Kidman, McKenzie, & McKenzie, 1999), Cumming and Ewing observed 250 parents across a variety of team sports, and while it was encouraging that the majority of verbal comments that parents made during the competitions were positive (47.2%) a high percentage were negative (34.5%). Similarly, in another study (Homan, 2006), maternal and paternal support of sports were correlated to youth enjoyment and continued involvement in sports. Despite the fact that maternal and paternal pressures themselves were not linked, youth perceived parental pressure to be of equal value suggesting that a parent's gender and the actual beliefs that parents value whether as a mother or father may not necessarily be a contributing factor in a child's enjoyment of and continued participation in sport. A child's perceptions of these beliefs and attitudes are a fundamental element (e.g., Bois, Sarrazin, Brustad, Chanal, & Trouilloud, 2005; Bray, Martin, & Widmeyer, 2000; Stein, Raedeke, & Glenn, 1999). Homan's results also uncovered a negative relationship between parental pressure and "likely continued involvement in school sports" (no page #, 2006).

Using a different approach by addressing the concerns that coaches held about parental involvement in youth sport, Gould, Lauer, Rolo, Jannes, and Pennisi (2006) surveyed the attitudes of 132 experienced, junior tennis coaches in the United States. Coaches believed that the majority of parents (almost 60%) were a positive influence (e.g., providing financial and emotional support). However, almost 36% also felt that over one-third of parents can negatively impact on their children by holding high expectations, being too ego-oriented (win-at-all-costs) or critical. The latter negative expectations appear to set parents up as perpetrators of negative behavior in the perceptions of some coaches which has the potential of filtering down to both youth and their parents (self-fulfilling prophecy). Such negative representation of parents by coaches reinforces the need to educate the latter—one goal of this book!

Generally, then, work in the area has supported the belief that many questions have yet to be explored with respect to such variables as the type of sport; level of competition; and qualities related to the child and parents such as gender, motivational orientation, perceived self competence, and attributions for success as well as the bi-directionality of parent-child interactions. In the interim, research has provided evidence for the positive effects of parental involvement in youth sport. This is indeed valuable information for all stakeholders.

MOTIVATION TO PARTICIPATE—WHAT ARE THE SOURCES?

We know from the earlier research literature in this area that children participate in sports primarily for fun and not necessarily to win (Gould, Feltz, & Weiss, 1985). However, what has been reported with regard to the possible conflict between the motivations parents hold for their children and the reasons why children themselves participate in sport? Naturally, a breakdown in shared goal orientations may result in increased tension between and for both parties. Of significance, in the long term, is 1) whether the motivational climate influences youth's continued participation, enjoyment, general attitude and feelings of personal success and competence, and 2) whether interventions are successful in conveying the message to parents that the less controlling they are perceived to be by their children the more positive the latters' experiences. Even research on elite athletes has shown that they can be task-oriented (process) rather than ego-oriented (winning at all costs, Burnett, 1998).

In a study by Givvin (2001) adolescent swimmers perceived their coaches and parents as holding similar motivational beliefs to their own, but this was not the case. The motivations parents hold for their child-athlete can be multi-faceted (Cummings & Ewing, 2002). They range from seeking such rewards as athletic scholarships, social status, the fame and fortune of being a professional athlete ("... less than one half of one percent of all high school athletes will ever become professional athletes", Cumming & Ewing, p. 3), and to satisfy unfulfilled dreams of their own. Murphy (1999) addressed at length the 'dark side' of youth sports. In his book, he described parents' over-identification with their children (Smoll's "reverse-dependency trap", Cumming & Ewing, p. 3) and the ego-oriented goals they held for them. What does the motivation-based research in this area reveal?

Investigating the relationships among variables, Gagne, Ryan and Bargmann (2003) used Self-determination Theory (SDT) as the basis for examining the motivational climate that adults created for 45, young female gymnasts (ages 7–18). They explored whether the influence of coaches and parents corresponded to the gymnasts' own psychological need for autonomy, competence and relatedness; motivation and well being. The SDT model has been tested in various physical activity milieu as well as academic ones (e.g., Baron & Sicoly, under review; Markland, Ryan, Tobin, & Rollnick, 2005; Pelletier, Fortier, Vallerand, & Brière, 2001; Pelletier et al., 1995; Vallerand & Losier, 1999). Using the model, researchers are able to examine the links between individual and/or situational factors, psychological needs of participants, levels of motivation, and behavior or emotion. In their work, Gagne, Ryan and Bargmann examined the nature of the motivational climate adults provided young athletes (e.g., intrinsically motivating or controlling) and its effect on well being (e.g., positive affect, vitality and self-esteem). The researchers expected that those gymnasts with more autonomous needs and self-determined motivations would exude qualities of positive well being regardless of the motivational orientation of their parents. The participants kept daily diaries indicating their motivation to attend practice, their evaluation of whether their needs were being met or not through their sport involvement, and their well being. For one month, they completed measures before and after 15 practices. For the purpose of the chapter, only results related to parents and coaches' influence will be reported. The Children's Perception Of Parents Scale (Grolnick et al. as cited in Gagne, Ryan, & Bargmann) and a modified version to measure coach autonomy support and involvement were used in the study. Results revealed a positive relationship between perceived parent autonomy support and identified (e.g., personally valuable) and intrinsic motivation (e.g., fun, interesting, challenging). Perceived parent involvement and both self-determined and extrinsic motivation were linked demonstrating that how children perceive their parent's support can be related to both self-regulatory motivations and external ones. Perceived coach autonomy support also corresponded to identified motivation and more self-determined motivation. Perceived parent involvement and coach autonomy support also were related to the number of practices attended. The researchers concluded that "the more autonomy supportive and involved parents and coaches were perceived to be by the gymnasts, the more autonomously motivated the gymnasts were" (Gagne, Ryan, & Bargmann, p. 385). Additionally, coach involvement was linked to feelings of self-esteem. Of significance, these findings confirmed the results of other work that demonstrated the positive effects that both parents and coaches can have on the motivation of young athletes. From a practical perspective, this study has uncovered the important link between the influence of both parents and coaches on athletes' feelings of autonomy and competence, levels of self-determination and in turn, feelings of self-esteem. An autonomy supportive environment, at least in this study, benefited the youth who participated. In other words, the more autonomous the athletes felt, in concert with corresponding support from parents and coaches, the more positive the experience. Gagne, Ryan and Bargmann's findings are indeed both positive and encouraging.

Similar in nature to the above work, Bois, Sarrazin, Brustad, Chanal, and Trouilloud (2005) used Reflective Appraisal Theory to investigate those factors that influence perceived competence. Reflective appraisal specifies how individuals incorporate the appraisals of others into their own perceptions of self. With regard to youth sport, using Reflective Appraisal Theory addresses the question of how young athletes' feelings of self are in fact influenced by their perceptions of how others feel about them. Children's integrating parental beliefs and values has surfaced as an important factor in the quest for understanding the various dimensions involved in the parent-youth athlete relationship. For example, if a child perceives that his mother holds positive feelings about his competence in a particular sport, the proposition is that the child will internalize these perceptions. Naturally, negative perceptions also have the potential of being assimilated by a child.

More specifically, Bois, Sarrazin, Brustad, Chanal, and Trouilloud (2005) examined the influence of children's reflected appraisals of their parents' judgments on their own self-appraisals of sport competence. To test their hypothesis, data was gathered on the parents' own appraisals of their children's competence, the athletes' reflected appraisals of their parents' beliefs, and the children's own appraisals. Gender effects of both parent and child also were examined. One hundred and forty-seven, Grade 6 children of equal gender (ages 10 – 13 years) and both of their parents participated in the yearlong study. With respect to gender, results indicated that parental appraisals of competence did not vary by gender of their child, nor did the reflected appraisals of the child vary by parent gender. In other words, there was no differentiation by the gender of either child or parent. Similar lack of gender effects were found in the work of Davison (Davison, 2004) who looked at the links between activity support of parents, siblings, and peers and general physical activity in a sample of adolescents. As pointed out by Davison, it often had been assumed that boys received more parental support for physical activity pursuits than girls. Her results underscored the importance of support from family and friends as a means of promoting physical activity with all children regardless of gender.

Bois, Sarrazin, Brustad, Chanal, and Trouilloud's (2005) findings supported the relationship between parental appraisals and children's reflected appraisals indicating that the children's perceptions of how their parents felt about their physical parents' beliefs were quite accurate. The researchers pointed out that their findings were controversial in comparison to other work that has revealed that individuals are not so accurate in making sense of how others perceive them. They partially attributed their findings to the age of the participants whose relationships with their parents were still very close. Results also indicated that the reflected appraisals of parents' attitudes about their children's physical competency had moderately positive effects on the children's self-appraisals. In other words, and worthy of note, there was some evidence that children internalized their parents' perceptions into their own constructions of self-competence. That the effects were only moderate can be interpreted as encouraging, or not, depending on whether one looks at the parent-child relationship in youth sport as being "half full" or "half empty". Interestingly, when reflected appraisals were controlled for, there was no significant relationship between parent appraisals and self-appraisals demonstrating the influence of reflective appraisals. The researchers concluded, however, that generally it is more than likely that significant others such as coaches, peers, teammates and others influence self-appraisals. Using ecologically based theory, future research should address the influence of these and other variables. The findings of Bois, Sarrazin, Brustad, Chanal, and Trouilloud's work were admittedly controversial in comparison to other research results. Their study did, however, add a more robust dimension to work in this area with its more complex design and analyses.

At the very least, parents should encourage their child-athletes in positive and healthy ways by, for example, lowering or setting realistic expectations and becoming more aware of the type of feedback they pass on to their children. Research directed at developmental differences as well as the influence of different sport milieu and levels of participation is needed. Concurrent with developmental theory on the nature of social relationships (e.g., Selman, 1980), it already appears that parental appraisals lose their influence as peers and coaches become more influential in the lives of youth.

Providing some insight with regard to the above assumption, Bray, Martin, and Widmeyer (2000) studied the link between what they called social evaluation concerns and competitive anxiety with 34 (19 male, 15 female) competitive skiers (mean age = 13.74). Citing past research that had already established this link, Bray, Martin, and Widmeyer sought to further understand the nature of the relationship by looking at the potentially different effects of social evaluation on cognitive (e.g., worry) and somatic (e.g., physiological arousal) anxiety. A "self-presentational approach" (Bray, Martin, & Widmeyer, p. 353) was the theoretical basis of their work. Basically, the assumption underlying this theory is that competitive anxiety may result from worrying about how others perceive you (social evaluative concerns). Worrying about negative evaluations is what causes anxiety. They hypothesized that social evaluative concerns about performance would have a stronger impact on cognitive than on somatic anxiety. Using a systems approach, they examined the source of social evaluative concerns—parents, fellow competitors, peers and strangers.

General evaluative concerns were measured by a modified version of the Fear of Negative Evaluation scale for children (FNE, La Greca et al. as cited in Bray, Martin, & Widmeyer, 2000). An example item includes, "... when you are skiing and other people are watching you... I worry about what other ski competitors think of me" (Bray, Martin, & Widmeyer, p. 355). To assess specific performance-related evaluative concerns, skiers were asked, "How important do you feel it is to ski well in a race when ____ (parents, friends, other competitors, or strangers) are watching you?" (Bray, Martin, & Widmeyer, p. 355). Martens Competitive State Anxiety Inventory-2 (CSAI-2, Martens et al. as cited in Bray, Martin, & Widmeyer) was used to measure competitive state anxiety. Results indicated that parents and strangers had significant influence on general evaluative concerns while friends and parents significantly affected performance-related evaluative concerns. The results reflecting parental influence are particularly informative in a developmental sense considering the fact that the skiers were teenagers. With respect to social evaluation and cognitive and somatic state anxiety, general evaluative concerns were significantly linked to both while performance-related evaluative concerns were correlated with cognitive anxiety. Further analyses linked general evaluations from friends and strangers with cognitive state anxiety and from fellow competitors and strangers with somatic anxiety. Of importance to sport competitive anxiety and the role of parents, the study revealed that both parents and friends influenced performance-related evaluative concerns resulting in cognitive anxiety. However, additional multiple regression analyses targeted only parents. Unfortunately, the researchers did not tease out the effects of gender. Despite certain acknowledged limitations of the study, some practical implications for youth sport were identified. The foremost implication of this research was that parents and coaches should be aware of the fact that young athletes do have social evaluative concerns in competitive situations that could lead to worry and fluctuations in performance. Furthermore, parents in particular appeared to be a major source of worry within this sample.

All in all, research on the effects of parents on youth sport has evolved significantly in the last decade. While we have a much better understanding of the nature of this relationship, we also have discovered that it is a very complex one. It would be most appropriate for future research to embrace developmentally sound, ecologically based and interactionist research. For example, work reported in this chapter has looked at the relationship between child-athletes appraisals of their parents' beliefs and the children's own competence and beliefs. In turn, we should be examining how the latter impacts on parents' beliefs and values consequently feeding back into the the cycle.

In their extensive review of parental involvement in youth sport, Fredricks and Eccles (2004) highlighted some implications for future work in this area that are worth sharing. First, research should go beyond examining the effects variable by variable (e.g., regression analysis), and use research techniques that explore the intricacies of effects both cumulatively and in interaction with each other. Fredricks and Eccles also called for the use of "alternative methodologies (p. 158), and encouraged investigating specific types of parental involvement beyond treating involvement as a generalized phenomenon. Finally, future research work should explore developmental differences, gender effects, ecological and interactionist perspectives and effects on diverse populations including special needs and at risk youth.

PROGRAMS FOR PARENTS

Sport-related organizations have made it their role to provide parents with workshops on fair play and proper conduct. A driving force behind the development of these educational experiences has been heightened awareness of cases of abusive behavior directed by parents toward athletes, coaches, referees and fellow spectators. Some examples of these organizations are provided at the end of the chapter. What follows is a brief summary of strategies for parents that one might find on theses organizations' websites.

SOME SPORTS-PARENTING TIPS (... "TIP OF THE ICEBERG")

1. LISTEN to your children, and discuss with them their feelings about being involved in what may be *your* chosen sport for them.
2. Insure that you know what your child's own goals are for their sport involvement.
3. Find and enroll in a program for sport parents (short of that, read what is available on the internet sites listed below). Become more literate about positive sport parenting.
4. Ask yourself what YOU are gaining from your child's involvement in sports. Be honest!!
5. Be "generous" about providing positive support to your child- athlete (emotional, functional and financial). Do not instill guilt regarding the time and money you invest.
6. Do not be judgmental or critical.
7. Do not overreact to mistakes. Learn to be calm. After all, sports are only games!
8. Commend participation not results.
9. Encourage your parks and recreation programs as well as local schools to hold fair play workshops for all stakeholders and to support a zero tolerance policy toward violence.

ORGANIZATIONS

1. National Alliance for Youth Sports (http://www.nays.org/pays/index.cfm)
2. American Youth Soccer Association (http://www.soccer.org)

3. SAFE KIDS (http://www.safekids.com, www.safekids.org, www.safekidscanada.ca, www.safekids.org.nz)

4. The Child and Adolescent Sport and Activity Lab (CASA. http://www.ualberta.ca/~nholt/)

5. Institute for the Study of Youth Sports (http://ed-web3.educ.msu.edu/ysi/)

CONCLUSION

The conundrum with respect to parental involvement in youth sport appears to be that individuals developing programs for youth must satisfy and respect parents' perceptions of the value of youth sport as ultimately the latter influence early youth participation while also attempting to meet the needs of young participants. A reasonable objective is to harmonize both parents' and young athletes' attitudes with a long term objective being to develop in youth a lifelong motivation to be active.

The issue of parental involvement is much more complex than it appears on the surface. It is not simply that parents have a negative or positive effect on their young athlete. From the ever-growing body of research in the area many variables appear to factor into the equation—perceived motivations and real motivations for success and involvement of both youth and their significant others; young athletes perceptions of the involvement, beliefs and values their parents, coaches, and fellow players hold; and developmental and gender differences. Researchers should be utilizing more complex models to determine the nature of these relationships.

Not all sports parents are bad! On reviewing the ever-increasing research on the effects of parental support on youth, despite all the negative hype, parents can provide positive support for their child-athlete. As socializing agents, parents have the potential of being positive role models who can instill in children healthy perceptions of their sport competence and confidence as well as inculcating in them the benefits of participation and being active. Recent work has confirmed earlier studies in the area (e.g., Brustad, 1993; Scanlan & Lewthwaite, 1986, 1985); nevertheless, the stereotypes of the 'raging' sport parent still prevail. Hopefully, through education, more research and the sharing of results to all members of the youth sport community, more positive messages not only will be conveyed, but also will be incorporated into parents' own sense of their influence. In time, through awareness, the image of the sport parent may take on new meaning.

REFERENCES

Barber, H., Sukhi, H., & White, S. (1999). The influence of parent-coaches on participant motivation and competitive anxiety in youth sport participants. *Journal of Sport Behavior, 22*(2), 162-181.

Baron, L., & Sicoly, F. (under review). A self-determination approach to understanding of psychological needs, motives and levels of activity at home, work and recreation.

Bois, J. E., Sarrazin, P. G., Brustad, R. J., Chanal, J. P., & Trouilloud, D. O. (2005). Parents' appraisals, reflected appraisals, and children's self-appraisals of sport competence: A yearlong study. *Journal of Applied Sport Psychology, 17*(273-289).

Braddock, L. L., & Petrie, T. A. (2005). *The relationships between parental personality factors of neuroticism and conscientiousness and goal orientations in girls' youth soccer.* Paper presented at the Association for the Advancement of Applied Sport Psychology. Vancouver, BC.

Bray, S. R., Martin, K. A., & Widmeyer, W. N. (2000). The relationship between evaluative concerns and sport competition state anxiety among youth skiers. *Journal of Sports Sciences, 18*(5), 353-361.

Brustad, R. J. (1993). Who will go out and play? Parental and psychological influences on children's attraction to physical activity. *Pediatric Exercise Science, 5,* 210-223.

Burnett, D. J. (1998). Coaching Youth Sports, parents' perspectives: Attitude in Youth Sports: Parents set the tone ("Hey, mom & dad, your attitude is showing!"). Retrieved 15/7/04, 2004, from http://www.courseware.vt.edu/users/rstratto/CVSarchive/ParentsNov98.html

Davison, K. (2004). Activity-related support from parents, peers, and siblings and adolescents' physical activity: Are there gender differences? *Journal of Physical Activity and Health, 1,* 363-376.

DeFrancesco, D., & Johnson, P. (1997). Athlete and parent perceptions in junior tennis. *Journal of sport Behavior, 20*(1), 29-36.

Docheff, D. M., & Conn, J. H. (2004). It's No Longer a Spectator Sport. *Parks & Recreation, 39*(3), 62-70.

Erin, H. (2005). Hockey-parent outbursts persist despite efforts. Retrieved January 18, 2005, from http//www.canada.com

Fredricks, J. A., & Eccles, J. S. (2004). Parental influences on youth involvement in sports. In M. R. Weiss (Ed.), *Developmental sport and exercise psychology: A lifespan perspective.* Morgantown, WV: Fitness Information Technology, Inc.

Gagne, M., Ryan, R. M., & Bargmann, K. (2003). Autonomy support and need satisfaction in the motivation and well-being of gymnasts. *Journal of Applied Sport Psychology, 15*(4), 372-390.

Givvin, K. B. (2001). Goal orientations of adolescents, coaches, and parents: Is there a convergence of beliefs? *The Journal of Early Adolescence, 21*(2), 228-248.

Gould, D., Feltz, D., & Weiss, M. (1885). Reasons for attrition in competitive youth swimming. *Journal of Sport Behavior, 5,* 155-165.

Gould, D., Feltz, D., & Weiss, M. (1985). Reasons for attrition in competitive youth swimming. *Journal of Sport Behavior, 5,* 155-165.

Gould, D., Lauer, L., Rolo, C., Jannes, C., & Pennisi, N. (2006). Understanding the role parents play in tennis success: a national survey of junior tennis coaches. *British Journal of Sports Medicine, 40*(7), 632-636.

Hedstrom, R., & Gould, D. (2004). *Research in youth sports: Critical issues status.* East Lansing, MI: Institute for the Study of Youth Sports.

Homan, G. (2006). Exploration of parent, 4-H volunteer advisor, and sports coach support and pressure on youth involved in 4-H and/or school sports. *Journal of Extension, 44*(1), 225-242.

Hoyle, R. H., & Left, S. S. (1997). The role of parental involvement in youth sport participation and performance. *Adolescence, 32*(125), 233-244.

Jambor, E. A. (1999). Parents as Children's Socializing Agents in Youth Soccer. *Journal of Sport Behavior, 22*(3), 350-361.

Kidman, L., McKenzie, A., & McKenzie, B. (1999). The nature and target of parents' comments during youth sport competitions. *Journal of Sport Behavior, 22*(1), 54-69.

Markland, D., Ryan, R. M., Tobin, V. J., & Rollnick, S. (2005). Motivational interviewing and self-determination theory. *Journal of Social and Clinical Psychology, 24*(6), 811-831.

Murphy, S. (1999). *The cheers and the tears--A healthy alternative to the dark side of youth sports today.* San Francisco: Jossey-Bass.

Nease, S. (Artist). (January 23, 2005). [cartoon].

Pelletier, L. G., Fortier, M. S., Vallerand, R. J., & Brière, N. M. (2001). Associations among perceived autonomy support, forms of self-regulation, and persistence: A prospective study. *Motivation and Emotion, 25*, 279-306.

Pelletier, L. G., Fortier, M. S., Vallerand, R. J., Tuson, K. M., Brière, N. M., & Blais, M. R. (1995). Toward a new measure of intrinsic motivation, extrinsic motivation, and amotivation in sports: The sport motivation scale (SMS). *Journal of Sport and Exercise Psychology, 17*, 35-53.

Scanlan, T., & Lewthwaite, R. (1985). Social psychological aspects of competition of male youth sports participants: III. Determinants of personal performance expectancies. *Journal of Sport Psychology, 7*, 389-399.

Scanlan, T., & Lewthwaite, R. (1986). Social psychological aspects of competition for male youth sports participants: IV. Predictors of enjoyment. *Journal of Sport Psychology, 8*, 25-35.

Selman, R. L. (1980). *The growth of interpersonal understanding.* New York: Academic Press.

Stein, G. L., Raedeke, T. D., & Glenn, S. D. (1999). Children's perceptions of parent sport involvement: It's not how much, but to what degree that's important. *Journal of Sport Behavior, 22*(4), 591-600.

Vallerand, R. J., & Losier, G. F. (1999). An integrated analysis of intrinsic and extrinsic motivation in sport. *Journal of Applied Sport Psychology, 11*, 142-169.

Weiss, M. R., & Fretwell, S. D. (2005). The parent-coach/child-athlete relationship in youth sport: Cordial, contentious, or conundrum? *Research Quarterly for Exercise and Sport, 76*(3), 286-305.

Chapter 2

YOUTH SPORT AND FAIR PLAY

The context in which sport is played can have a lasting effect on a child's development including their moral character. In fact, 90% of respondents to a U.S. survey conducted in 1999 believed that sport teaches children good sportspersonship (Citizenship Through Sports Alliance as cited in Gano-Overwaya, Guivernau, Magyar, Waldrond, & Ewing, 2005). Whether a child watches a sport played by others, live or on television, or participates themselves, how the sport is played including the behavior witnessed in the stands, on the field/ice and behind the bench, has an impact on their perceptions of what is right and wrong, acceptable or unacceptable behavior. These perceptions contribute to shaping a developing child's moral sense that can carry into other venues of life.

As May (2001, see for a review of the earlier literature) pointed out, the win at all costs attitude that pervades the sports world has created a contradiction or "sticky situation" (p. 372) for participants when society's definition of fair play is put to test within a competitive environment. One would think that this dilemma would be particularly difficult for the developing child whose sense of right and wrong can easily be swayed by coaches, parents, and peers. May suggested that the root of unsportspersonlike behavior (e.g., cheating) evolved from the pressure to win, the commercialization of sport, and the reward structure that envelops sport (and for that matter society) at all levels. A report for the Canadian Centre for Ethics in Sport (CCES, 2002) emphasized a similar view of the effects of the competitive nature, commercialization and emphasis on the entertainment value of sport on standards of fair play. Obviously, unsportspersonlike behavior is not limited to athletes.

The CCES carried out its own public opinion survey. They questioned individuals who were 18 years and older in order to examine their attitudes towards the ethics of sport and the value of sport for the developing child. The objective was to gather enough data that would aid policy makers and those who design interventions at the general and educational level. Most developed countries have similar federally funded programs. Results of the CCES survey uncovered the fundamental role that sport plays in Canadian society ("only the family is more apt to be considered as influential in shaping the development of the younger generation", p. 3). Respondents saw sport as a "critically important" venue for promoting positive values in youth (e.g., teamwork, commitment, fair play, respect for others) yet survey results indicated that these objectives were judged as not being met. The most serious problem facing community sport as seen by the respondents was the focus on winning. More extensive analysis uncovered some age, socioeconomic status, and geographical differences.

It is evident that youth sport plays a dominant role in child development. The abundance of research on sportspersonship in sport speaks to this influence.

The purpose of this chapter is to familiarize the reader with the main theoretical positions that have driven research in the area. For an historical look at character education, particularly in Britain, readers are referred to Theodoulides and Armour (2001/02). The goal of this chapter is to present not only the research findings, but also the implications of research results for athletes, coaches, parents, teachers and anyone working with youth. The results have practical import in terms of the psychological and sociological environment that young athlete participate in. For example, research has demonstrated that the goal orientation displayed by both coaches and parents can affect a player's attitudes about fair play and resultant behavior in a sports setting (e.g., Boixados, Cruz, Torregrosa, & Valiente, 2004; Lemyre, Roberts, & Ommundsen, 2002; Miller, Roberts, & Ommundsen, 2004). Furthermore, a study carried out in Greece with participants ranging in age from 14 to 49 years, revealed that the development of moral reasoning in sport holds no boundaries with respect to type of sport, levels and years of participation (Proios, Doganis, & Athanailidis, 2004). This is valuable information for those involved in youth sport and interested in intervention work with youth.

Participation in sport can contribute to the psychosocial development of a child including their ability to cooperate with others, share, negotiate and generally participate with a sense of fair play toward both their own teammates and their opponents (Lemyre, Roberts, & Ommundsen, 2002). These are some of the positive virtues of sportspersonship. Lemyre, Roberts, and Ommundsen professed that research and well-known examples from the sport world, have proven not only that "sports builds character" (p. 120), but also that sport can encourage antisocial behavior. There is obviously worldwide concern about the ethics of sport including youth sport. The Canadian Center for Ethics in Sport, the Council of Europe, Character Counts Coalition in the United States, and the Australian Sports Commission are examples of federal bodies that have outlined a code of ethics not only for players, but also officials, coaches, spectators, administrators, and parents. Individual teams also have developed their own code of ethics.

DEFINING SPORTSPERSONSHIP

It is difficult to precisely define the concept of "sportspersonship". Feezel has provided the following definition: "a sport participant manifests sportspersonship when he or she tries to play well and strive for victory and defeat" (as cited in Lemyre, Roberts, & Ommundsen, 2002, p. 121). It also has been defined as "... the virtue of coordinating the play impulse with the competitive one in light of moral goals" (Shields and Bredemeier as cited in Lemyre et al., p. 121). More simply, "sportspersonship is characterized by notions of civility and is a matter of being good (character) and doing right (action) in sports" (Grough as cited in May, 2001, p. 373).

Vallerand and Losier (1994) have operationally defined sportspersonship from a social psychological perspective by classifying it into five dimensions: 1) full commitment toward sport participation, 2) respect for social conventions, 3) respect and concern for the rules and officials, 4) true respect and concern for the opponent, and 5) a negative approach to sportspersonship. Boixados, Cruz, Torregrosa, and Valiente (2004) designed an instrument called the Fair Play Attitudes Scale (EAF) which measures characteristics of fair play similar to those delineated by Vallerand: 1) rough play and cheating, 2) the importance of winning, and 3) enjoyment. These elements of sports participation have been shown to be heavily linked to the motivational orientation of sports participants and resultant moral behavior in sport settings.

APPROACHES TO RESEARCH IN THE AREA

Much of the research in the area of sportspersonship or the morality of youth sport has embraced two particular theoretical positions or combinations of the two --Achievement Goal Theory (Nicholls, 1989) and the more constructivist-developmental work of Haan (1991) and Kohlberg (1981, 1984). The former incorporates motivation theory and more specifically issues of goal orientation (task- or ego- oriented) while the latter complements Kohlberg's developmental stages of moral development, Bandura's social cognitive learning theory and Vygotsky's social constructivist position by placing the emphasis on the effects of one's social-cognitive environment on one's beliefs about what constitutes moral behavior in sport (Bandura, 1973, 1986; Vygotsky, 1962; Wertsch, 1985). Through sport participation, children both model those around them, and more cognitively speaking, construct knowledge of moral beliefs and values throughout their development. Regardless of which theoretical position is supported, coaches, parents, peers and others who are significant participants in the dialogue with children define the *moral atmosphere* within which youth sport is played.

MOTIVATIONAL APPROACHES

Situational factors such as motivational climate as well as individual goal orientations (and the interaction between the two) also have been the focus of sportspersonship research (Gano-Overwaya, Guivernau, Magyar, Waldrond, & Ewing, 2005; Ommundsen, Roberts, Lemyre, & Treasure, 2003). The motivational approach to studying sportspersonship and moral functioning was the theoretical framework used by such researchers in the area as, for example, Boixados, Cruz, Torregrosa and Valiente (2004); Duda, Olson and Templin (1991); Kavussanu and Roberts (2001a); Lemyre, Roberts and Ommundsen (2002); and Roberts (2001). As Boixados, Cruz, Torregrosa and Valiente pointed out, the strength of research results in the area of goal orientation and moral behavior in sport has been supported by research efforts carried out across multiple cultures. Drawing on Achievement Goal Theory (Nicholls, 1989), research using the achievement goal approach has examined the relationships between goal orientation (task- or ego-oriented) and moral behavior (e.g., cheating) in sport. In Nicholl's view, one's goal orientation determines what one considers suitable behavior in a particular situation. According to Nicholls, for "ego-oriented individuals.... When winning is everything, it is worth doing anything to win" (as cited in Stephens & Kavanagh, 2003, p. 110). On the other hand, task-oriented athletes show more respect for the rules and their opponents. Essentially, research using Achievement Goal Theory as a theoretical base has attempted to make sense of an athlete's behavior in sport by examining what motivates them to participate in the sport (e.g., to win, to have fun, to get into shape, to violate others).

Other variables, such as perceived ability and social goal orientations also have been factored into the research equation to further understand the nature of moral functioning in sport (e.g., Boixados, Cruz, Torregrosa, & Valiente, 2004; Lemyre, Roberts, & Ommundsen, 2002; Stuntz & Weiss, 2003). For example, those with low perceived ability may resort to inappropriate means of competing to compensate for lack of skill. Essentially, ego-oriented players perceive personal competence in a competitive setting differently than those who are task-oriented. The former have a more difficult time losing. Their 'egos' or perceptions of competence are tied into the outcome of a competition. As a result, they may seek different means to win, particularly if they are not skilled, that do not necessarily include effort, persistence or fair play -- qualities possessed by more task-oriented individuals. Roberts (2001) suggested that perceived ability is over-rated when it comes to success for the majority of sport competitors and often leads to maladaptive behaviors. For example, even at the professional level, there is evidence of the 'underdog' defeating a more skilled team through hard work. In addition, Achievement Goal Theory underscores the influence that significant others have in moral decision making (Shields & Bredemeier, 1995; Stuntz & Weiss, 2003; Weiss & Smith, 2002).

Lemyre, Roberts and Ommundsen (2002) investigated the relationship between achievement goal orientation (ego- or task-) and moral functioning in youth soccer while also exploring the effects of perceived ability as a mediating variable. Participants were males ranging in age from 13 to 15. Goal orientation was measured using the Perception of Success Questionnaire (POSQ) while perceived ability (e.g., "How good a soccer player are you?") was evaluated using items from the Intrinsic Motivation Inventory. The researchers used Vallerand's Multidimensional Orientations Sportspersonship Scale (MSOS) to measure sportspersonship (e.g., "I respect the rules even when the opponent cheats" or "When the opponent injures himself I do not take advantage of the situation").

Consistent with other work, correlations revealed that goal orientation was meaningfully linked to sportspersonship contributing to 57% of the variance. Further, high task/low ego-orientation was positively related to the sportspersonship dimensions. A combination of high ego-orientation with task-orientation led to mixed results on the sportspersonship measures. Analyses uncovered positive effects of perceived ability and negative effects of ego-orientation on all four dimensions of sportspersonship measured by the MSOS (full commitment toward sport participation, respect for social conventions, respect for rules and officials, and respect and concern for the opponent). In combination, however, ego-orientation and perceived ability revealed a significant, but negative, relationship with regard to "respect for rules and officials". Those players with low ego-orientation and high perceived ability were more "respectful of rules and officials". However, perceived ability did not appear to moderate goal orientation with reference to "respect for one's opponent". More importantly, the results have implications for sportspersonship in youth sport. As Lemyre, Roberts and Ommundsen (2002) have suggested, what is key for parents and coaches is knowing that a young player whose main goal is to win (ego orientation) and who may be lacking in skills (low ability) may resort to breaking rules (e.g., cheat) and harassing officials in order to be successful. As has been proven over numerous studies, an ego orientation is not a trait conducive to displaying sportspersonship in sport. It therefore rests on the shoulders of parents, coaches and teachers to instill more task-oriented goal orientations in youth through modeling such an orientation in sport and life and by creating task-oriented environments for sport participation.

In their study, Boixados, Cruz, Torregrosa, and Valiente (2004) investigated the links between perceived motivational climate (Perceived Motivational Climate Scale), ability (Conceptions of Perceived Ability Scale), satisfaction (Satisfaction/Interest Scale) and fair play (Fair Play Attitudes Scale) in male soccer players ranging in age from 10 to 14 who averaged 5 years of competitive sport. By examining perceived motivational climate (i.e., if it was perceived by the players that the coach has set up a mastery learning environment), Boixados, Cruz, Torregrosa, and Valiente expanded upon previous work. Significant findings supported what the researchers labeled as "logical patterns" (p. 307)—a task-oriented environment was positively related to satisfaction, self-referenced perceived ability, winning (small correlation) and enjoyment (small correlation) and negatively related to rough play and cheating while an ego-oriented environment was positively linked to rough play and cheating (small correlation), winning, and slightly, yet significantly, associated with satisfaction. Additional analysis revealed that a high task-involving climate was linked to higher scores on satisfaction and perceived ability while the opposite was true of a low task-involving climate. Also, as expected, a high ego-involving climate was associated with winning. Enjoyment surfaced in a high task- and low ego-involving climate with the opposite true of the low task- and high ego-oriented cohort who condoned cheating and rough play. Essentially and for practical purposes, Boixados et al.'s research underscored the fact that a high task-involving and low ego-involving climate sets young athletes up for more satisfying experiences, more positive perceptions of their own ability, and an attitude that embraces sportspersonship. A winning attitude, strong perceived ability and moderate satisfaction was exemplary of those who were both ego-involving and task-involving. Similar findings regarding the interaction between goal orientation and motivational climate have been reported by Treasure, Roberts and Standage (as cited in Roberts, 2001). Despite uncovering findings consistent with comparable work, Boixados, Cruz, Torregrosa and Valiente mentioned that much of the variance in their study was unexplained. They addressed the need for sustained research on the psychological and other factors that play a role in the interrelationships between perceived motivational climate, children's satisfaction and enjoyment, and moral behavior. As stressed in this chapter, such information has practical import depending on the level of play and goals of the coach.

In Duda, Olson and Templin's (1991b) research in the area, unsportspersonlike play, cheating and aggression positively correlated with low task- and high ego-orientation leading one to believe that goal orientation can mediate moral behavior in sport at any age. Similarly, Stephens and Bredemeier (1996) studied the behavior of young, female soccer players, and reported that those who were more ego-oriented exuded more aggressive and unsportspersonlike behavior. As well, Kavussanu and Roberts (2001b) found that ego-oriented players justified intentionally injuring their opponents! In essence, players high in ego-orientation appear to adopt a "win at all costs" attitude.

A social psychological and motivational approach that embraces Self-determination Theory was the foundation of research by Vallerand and Losier (1994). They uncovered a relationship between early self-determined sport motivation and later sportspersonship. Those who at the outset of the study were more intrinsically motivated to participate in their sport exemplified qualities of fair play five months later. Chantal and Bernache-Assollant (2003) replicated Vallerand and Losier's study with a mixed sample (17 female and 24 male students and a mean age of 20.9 years) using a time lag of one year. They expected positive relationships between early self-determined sport motivation and later sportspersonship values. Using the Sport Motivation Scale, participants indicated the source of their sport motivation (i.e., from amotivation to intrinsic motivation). Sportspersonship was measured using the Sportspersonship Orientation Scale (MSOS). Data on gender revealed that the women held moderately more, yet significantly different, sportspersonship qualities than the men. As well, and in support of their expectations and Vallerand and Losier's finding, they uncovered a positive relationship between self-determined sport motivation and sportspersonship orientations. These relationships also were stable over time. If the goal is to create youth sport environments that exude positive values, the results of this and Vallerand and Losier's work on self-determination and sportspersonship underscore the benefits of creating a youth sport atmosphere that satisfies needs for intrinsic motivation (e.g., fun, learning experience, self-regulation) over external rewards and control. Practically speaking, however, in the competitive environment of sport, this may be an unattainable objective. It is a matter of education and changes in attitude for all involved stakeholders including young athletes.

Social goal orientation also has been thought to mediate one's general goal orientation in sport (Stuntz & Weiss, 2003). Sport participants have been shown to not only strive to win (ego-oriented) or do as well as they can (task-oriented), but also to be motivated by social approval or what Self-determination theorists (e.g., Deci & Ryan, 1985) have labeled relatedness or connection with others. Both close relationships with teammates and/or coaches can play a significant role as already evinced by the goal orientation research introduced at the beginning of the chapter. Stuntz and Weiss have reviewed in detail the literature on social relationships in youth sport including some of the more general theories on peer relations, friendship, and social support. However, as they have pointed out, the relationship between social goal orientation and sportspersonlike behavior has not been put to the test within the sport domain except as related to aggressive acts. Supporting the latter research direction, Stuntz and Weiss examined the interactions of social goal orientations, the impact of peers and sportspersonship. Their premise was that moral beliefs and social goal orientation would be mediated by the values held by peers. They used an achievement goal orientation measure adapted from the TEOSQ (the Task and Ego Orientation Questionnaire) to evaluate social goal orientations (e.g., friendship, peer acceptance, and coach praise) as well as sport-related scenarios designed to judge moral reasoning and perspective taking. Participants included 406 middle school students (248 girls, M age = 13.01). The scenarios were modified to evaluate the influence of the moral attitudes of peers and/or best friend towards physical unsportspersonlike behavior. Stuntz and Weiss not only revealed that social goal orientations were in fact distinct from goal orientations and influenced moral attitudes, but also that the forms of social orientation (e.g., coach praise, friendship, and group acceptance) were quite distinct from each other. Also, the relationship between goal orientation and unsportspersonlike beliefs corroborated other research findings (e.g., Duda, Olson, & Templin, 1991a; Kavussanu & Roberts, 2001b; Lemyre, Roberts, & Ommundsen, 2002). Gender differences also surfaced. Essentially, the researchers demonstrated that both interpersonal and situational features could influence one's impressions of fair play within a youth sport venue.

Having emphasized the need for research on goal orientations, sportspersonship, females and teams, Gano-Overwaya, Guivernau, Magyar, Waldrond, and Ewing (2005) investigated these links with female volleyball players (M age = 15.12). Respect was the sportspersonship dimension studied. The researchers viewed respect as a proximal component of sportspersonship compared to previous research that considered respect for the game and opponents as distally related. Dispositional goal perspectives (TEOSQ), perceptions of motivational climate (PMCSQ-2, Perceived Motivational Climate in Sport Questionnaire), and sportspersonship orientations (MSOS) were measured. The players held high task orientations and moderate ego orientations which also matched their perceptions of the motivational environment. Results indicated a high level of respect for the game and moderate levels for their opponent that were mediated by goal orientation and motivational climate (i.e., the more task-oriented, the higher the level of respect). Both task orientation and a task-oriented motivational environment moderated high ego-oriented perceptions of respect for the game. Members of the same team held comparable opinions of the motivational climate. Generally, the participants in this study had respect for the game and their opponents. Gano-Overwaya, Guivernau, Magyar, Waldrond, and Ewing suggested that gender differences in the results could have been attributed to an ethic of care more characteristic of females. Bredemeier, Weiss, Shields, and Cooper (1986) and Bredemeier (1985) already had demonstrated that boys were more tolerant of aggressive behavior than girls in their investigations of 'sport morality'. Similar gender disparities have been uncovered in other work (e.g., Duda, Olson, & Templin, 1991a; Kavussanu & Roberts, 2001b; see Miller, Roberts, & Ommundsen, 2005 for a review).

In their work, Miller, Roberts, and Ommundsen (2005) uncovered significant gender variations in perceptions of motivational climate (mastery versus performance), moral functioning (judgment, reasoning, intention, behavior), moral atmosphere (teammates, coach) and legitimacy of injurious acts. They attributed the disparity between males and females as differences in sport socialization between the sexes (e.g., perception of what competition is). Their finding that moral cognitions and behavior have an impact on athletes' perceptions of the moral atmosphere created by the coach was a valuable discovery. The take-home message to coaches is to discuss with players goals (hopefully task-oriented), and to make their values and judgments with respect to success and failure very clear to players in both actions and words! Additionally, if there are indeed differential perceptions of sportspersonship by girls and boys, coaches, parents and fellow players (particularly in mixed game situations) should be aware of these disparate attitudes and behavior.

SOCIAL-CONSTRUCTIVIST AND DEVELOPMENTAL APPROACHES

Social constructivist approaches to sportspersonlike behavior have their root in developmental theory. Thankfully, this theoretical stance has been embraced in youth sport research in recent years. Essentially, studies have investigated the role that coaches, parents, teammates and the general mores of a team play in a child's construction of the concept of sportspersonship and resultant behavior in game situations. Much of this research has been based on moral constructs and the stage theories developed by Kohlberg (1981, 1984) and Haan (1991). Children's interpretation of moral dilemmas has been the methodology of choice in this line of research although Kavussanu, Seal, and Philips (in press) more recently used

Bandura's social cognitive theory of morality as the basis for carrying out observations of both pro- and anti-social behavior of adolescent, male soccer players.

Basically, Kohlberg (1981, 1984) held the view that the development of moral reasoning in children is both stage like in nature and linked to perceptions of and behavior toward 'justice'--right and wrong (keep in mind that his participants were male). Accordingly, the developing child moves from egocentric thinking about justice (preconventional stage) to a more differentiated and social perspective of moral reasoning (conventional and post conventional stages). Gilligan (Gilligan, 1982) expanded on Kohlberg's developmental work. She discovered that care as well as justice factored into female thinking about moral issues. What ties together Kohlberg and Gilligan's thinking is the Piagetian notion that self-oriented reasoning becomes more outer-directed through development. Being aware of these developmental shifts in thinking about morality is important for those working with youth as it provides a basis for understanding the moral thoughts and actions of children. Developmental work in the area also indicates the need for developing age-appropriate interventions. Haan's thinking about moral action is more social-constructivist in nature. Borrowing from Vygotsky (Vygotsky, 1962), she attributes moral action to the dialectic the individual holds with significant others within their environment. Some researchers who have explored the moral qualities inherent to youth sport have supported this perspective (e.g., see May, 2001; Shields & Bredemeier, unknown).

Bandura's (1973; 1986) cognitive social learning is included in this section despite its roots in behaviorism and learning theory. Earlier work on moral behavior in youth sport focused on modeling and reinforcement of aggressive acts (see Stuart, 2003, for a review of earlier literature). Yet, Bandura's current thinking has been cognitive in nature. His view of learning involves both observing others and mental processing (e.g., sensory processing, coding, rehearsal) by the child as s/he makes sense of the acts of others and decides whether to incorporate these behaviors into his/her own repertoire. Social interactions play an important role in cognition.

With social constructivist theory as the foundation of his work, May (2001) used an ethnographic approach (participant observation) to investigate the effects of social context on the sportspersonship attitudes of a group of male, high school basketball players. The defining feature of this research, and what made it social constructivist in nature, was May's proposition that individuals 'construct' the moral sense of their environment through interaction with others. In other words, an athlete's interactions with others and the sport-related situations in which these interactions take place influences not only one's sense of right and wrong in that context, but also how one might cross over to what Murphy (1999) called the dark side of youth sports.

An assistant coach, May (2001) witnessed a head coach's instilling in his players the virtues of winning by using personal recollections as well as references to such renowned coaches as Vince Lombardi. A "you gotta do what it takes to win" (May, p. 381) attitude resulted in athletes' resorting to such unsportspersonlike behavior as trash talking or elbowing opponents. As May so aptly expressed it, the coach "compromised levels of sportsmanship for victory" (p. 381). Basically, the coach helped define the moral belief system of the team through his interactions with the players. The players constructed their sense of how to behave on the court through the social context established and exuded by their coach.

Guivernau and Duda (2002) examined the relationship between moral orientation and female and male soccer players' likelihood to aggress (SLA) in competition. Social constructivist in nature, their research aligned with other work on aggression as an indicator of moral reasoning and behavior within the sport context (e.g., Shields & Bredemeier, 2001; Stephens & Kavanagh, 2003). Responses to sport-related moral dilemmas, and in turn, where participants were positioned developmentally as seen through their responses to these dilemmas, had been the methodology of choice for these researchers. The participants in Guivernau and Duda's study ranged in age from 13 to 19 years, and had played the game for 8 to 10 years. They investigated both who was most influential in shaping the athletes' orientations and gender differences in perceptions of a team's moral atmosphere. They also explored the interconnectedness between sport involvement and lower levels of moral reasoning (the latter being a likely reason for aggressive tendencies by sport participants) as well as gender differences in moral behavior. They found that males were influenced by team norm and perceived ability while girls by team norm and perceptions of their coach's mastery orientation. Guivernau and Duda emphasized the impact of the social context of sport. To them, the latter provided players with opportunities to construct a sense of right and wrong. Guivernau and Duda anticipated that coaches would have the most influence on moral orientation and that male athletes not only would hold higher scores on the SLA, but also that they would believe that their team norm encouraged a more aggressive approach.

They had the players complete a modified version of the Judgments about Moral Behavior in Youth Sport Questionnaire – a measure that uses moral dilemma scenarios to examine attitudes towards aggression. They asked players to rate whom they perceived as influencing their likelihood to aggress -- best friend, most popular player, team captain, best player, coach and parents. The players also completed a modified version of the Perceived Norms Questionnaire (TNQ). The latter measured their perceptions of team norms concerning aggression (e.g., did they feel that their teammates, coaches or parents would violate rules in order to win?). Significant differences between males and females in the perceived norms for cheating over losing were cause for analyzing the results by gender. However, no gender differences surfaced with respect to likelihood to aggress (SLA) in their study. Supporting earlier work, a link between perceived moral norm and SLA emerged. In other words, attitudes toward moral behavior in game situations were influenced by what the players sensed were the team norm. This phenomenon was particularly pronounced in female players' whose self-described likelihood toward unsportspersonlike behavior was related to their perceptions of their teammates' unfair play. Guivernau and Duda interpreted the influence of teammates as being typical for this age group. Adolescents tend to rely on their peers as models of behavior and sources of judgment. Regardless, and coaches take note, in this study, coaches surfaced as having the most influence on aggressive behavior despite gender.

Combining Achievement Goal Theory and using moral dilemmas, Stephens and Kavanagh (2003) carried out a similar study to that of Guivernau and Duda (2002). Participants were adolescent, male hockey players ranging in age from 9 to 18 years. The players averaged eight years of hockey experience. As a primary goal, they evaluated the effect of moral environment on the players SLA (self-described tendencies to aggress) and their motivation for doing so (goal orientation). They assessed goal orientation (TEOSQ), perceived goal orientation of the coach (TEOSQ_PPC) and attitudes about lying, cheating or hurting an opponent (Judgements About Moral Behavior in Youth Questionnaire, JAMBYSQ). The TEOSQ and JAMBYSQ were adapted for hockey (e.g., "I feel most successful in hockey when..." Stephens and Kavanaugh, p. 112). Using the JAMBYSQ, they asked study participants for their responses to a hockey-specific moral dilemma. Consistent with other studies, team norm had the most influence on SLA. Dividing the sample into elite and recreational teams, team norm influenced the more elite players tendencies toward aggression (34% of the variance) while for the more recreational hockey players, both team norms and an ego orientation were influential (23% and 2% of the variance respectively). The more ego-oriented recreational players were more likely to aggress. Elite team members identified their teammates as more accepting of antagonistic behavior on the ice, and perceived their coaches as more ego-oriented. It seems reasonable that a 'win at all costs attitude' would motivate the more elite teams, and would trigger an ego orientation with its resultant unsportspersonlike qualities.

Stuart (2003) did not support the use of moral dilemmas in assessing children's moral reasoning in youth sport as she understood the possible link between reading comprehension skills and children's moral reasoning scores. From her perspective, using adult-developed, hypothetical dilemmas was not a valid approach to understanding a child's ability to discern right from wrong. Stuart supported the use of realistic and child-centered concerns related to sport as a means of evaluating moral reasoning. She borrowed from Rest's (as cited in Stuart) four-component approach to studying determinants of moral behavior The components include: identifying a moral issue in a situation, and awareness of one's actions on others (Component 1), moral reasoning or deciding how to act on a moral issue (Component 2), prioritizing one's values when faced with a moral issue (Component 3), and resultant behavior (Component 4). The components are not linear, but rather dynamic and interactive. According to Stuart, most of the research in the area has focused on Component 2, moral reasoning, rather than on Component 1, incidents children themselves perceive to be moral dilemmas they actually face within the context of sport. Component 1 served as the foundation of Stuart's investigation. She wanted to hear the 'voices' of youth rather than utilize what she identified as artificial and adult-conceived dilemmas. The goal of Stuart's study, then, was to investigate children's self-identified moral issues in sport, and using Turiel's model (as cited in Stuart), to assess whether these self-identified issues could be classified as either moral (honesty, fairness and concern for others), conventional (social norms) or psychological/personal (possible sources of conflict with, for example, parents). Using Rest's definition of Component 1, Stuart interviewed youth involved in competitive sport as to what they perceived as problematic issues in their sport (7 boys and 8 girls, mean age = 11.6). She probed their responses, and invited them to write about the problem including the individuals involved. Using an inductive technique, Stuart teased out themes from their written work. Three main ones surfaced—adult actions, negative game behavior, and negative team behavior. Coaches' and parents' behavior, disrespect for fair play and physical harm, fighting at practices and dishonesty of team members were concerns held by the participants. Interestingly, she conceded that these "self-identified issues both confirmed and expanded upon the content found in hypothetical moral dilemmas in sport" (p. 445). However, as she elaborated, the self-identified moral issues expressed by the children also unearthed moral issues beyond game situations. They included those that the participants experienced in practices, pre- and post-competition, and at home. That the children saw adults as playing a leading role in setting the moral stage not only confirmed previous research, but also touched on the importance of adults' developing awareness of how influential they can be. Finally, Stuart's focusing on children's own perceptions and the qualitative nature of her work are both worthy considerations for future research methodology in this area.

Equally aware of the disadvantages of using moral dilemmas to study sportspersonlike behavior within the youth sport context and using qualitative methodology in the form of video analysis, Kavussanu, Seal, and Philips (in press) carried out a developmentally based study designed to directly observe behavior on the soccer field. Bandura's social cognitive theory of morality served as the theoretical basis for this study. For Kavussanu, Seal, and Philips, the consequences rather than the intentions of a player's actions defined moral behavior. Prosocial behavior was classified as helping or benefiting another. A wonderful example took place at the 2006 Winter Olympics when a Norwegian coach handed a pole to a Canadian cross country skier who had broken her's during an event. This prosocial act not only resulted in a silver medal for Canada, but also disadvantaged his own team. Antisocial behavior was behavior that harmed or disadvantaged an opponent. Kavussanu, Seal, and Philips also looked at developmental differences in pro- and anti-social behavior across three age groups—ages 12-13, 14-15, and 16-17. They hypothesized that with increased age players would exhibit less prosocial and more antisocial behavior. They also examined developmental shifts in goal orientation and motivational climate and resultant interactions between these two variables. Video analysis was used to assess behavior. Goal orientation and motivational climate were evaluated using standard measures used in other work (e.g., Perception of Success Questionnaire, Perceived Motivational Climate in Sport Questionnaire)

Overall, results revealed a greater incidence of antisocial behaviors. As well, in support of their expectations, significant age level differences surfaced with the older players exhibiting less prosocial and more antisocial behavior than the younger ones. The older the player, the more they perceived a performance- over mastery-oriented climate in their team. However, when goal orientation was factored into the analyses, age did not have a significant effect. In other words, a "mastery climate with ego orientation or performance climate, and task with ego orientation" (Kavussanu, Seal, & Philips, in press, p. 21) mediated age differences. Interestingly, the relationship between reported and observed behavior was stronger with antisocial over prosocial behavior. The researchers urged caution in interpreting these findings, as the number of prosocial acts was small. On further analysis, a mastery climate significantly predicted prosocial behavior (26% of variance) while a combination of mastery climate and ego orientation significantly correlated with antisocial behavior (37% of variance). Again, these findings have important implications for how players perceive the general motivational climate set up by the coach and resultant impact on behavior. It would be prudent of coaches to examine whether they establish a "sport for fun" as opposed to "win at all costs" atmosphere for their young players.

Supporting an ecological approach to moral understanding (e.g., Bronfenbrenner, 2005) while questioning structural developmental perspectives to moral development, Shields and Bredemeier (2001) expressed the view that moral judgment also develops through interaction with one's environment. Sport provides a unique setting that tests a child's moral beliefs in ways that may not be tested in other contexts. In other words, according to Shields and Bredemeier, moral reasoning is not only a developmental process, but also a dynamic one dictated by the requirements of the environment in which a child participates. In support of this proposition and demonstrating the distinctive moral context of sport, Bredemeier and Shields (2001) not only found that both college age basketball players and swimmers used less sophisticated thinking about moral dilemmas in sport than nonathletes, but also that reasoning about moral questions in sport was significantly less differentiated than that of reasoning about general life dilemmas ("bracketed morality", Bredemeier & Shields, 1986).

As they suggested, one can be a 'nice guy' in everyday life and a 'madman' once the clock starts. They labeled moral reasoning in sport "game reasoning". Their research uncovered the egocentric nature of sport reasoning which sets it apart from everyday thinking. Goal orientation and the context of competitive sport appear to be inter-related constructs. It might be interesting to examine whether type of sport also moderates goal orientations and "game reasoning".

IMPLICATIONS OF THE RESEARCH

Research over the last few decades has been quite definitive about coaches' influencing the values and beliefs held by young athletes. Research already has and must continue to embrace a variety of theoretical positions (e.g., social constructivist, ecological, social learning and developmental) in order to tease out those factors that are most influential in children's developing their own models of fair play. As evinced by the results of research in this area, the amount of variance attributable to predictor variables (e.g., team norm, ego orientation) has been rather small. The chapter on parent involvement in youth sport highlights the influence that parents play while much of the research in the area of fair play and youth sport focuses primarily on the role of the coach and teammates. While the commercial side of youth sport is discussed in this book from the perspective of mass media's influence on consumer behavior, there is little doubt that the media and sport-related role models highlighted through the media help shape children's sense of right and wrong. This topic is wide open to further investigation. Continued research in the area must be developmental and possibly longitudinal in nature while also embracing all ability and competitive levels if we are to understand with more confidence the roots of moral behavior in youth sport venues.

There is room for more extensive research in the area of fair play and youth sport (as well as PE). If coaches, teachers, parents, peers, the media and the larger culture hold similar attitudes toward achievement, what kind of role models and values are youth exposed to? Moreover, the research suggests that youth sport programs should encourage children to assume more task-oriented orientations to sport participation if fair play is truly a goal. This objective only can be accomplished if the 'actors' involved project and hold such moral orientations themselves. As suggested, type of sport (competitive, in-school, recreational) and different sports are factors that need to be clarified as related to this issue. Research has been moving in the right direction as more social/ecological factors involved in team versus individual sport are being examined. The door is widening for further investigation as youth take up alternative sports and the lines of gender-specific sports become more blurred. In fact, Kavussanu, Seal, and Philips' (in press) alluded to age-related shifts in thinking and acting morally in sport. Their results support existing developmental theory implying that further research and intervention work targeted at younger athletes should be carried out if the goal of youth sport is to promote a safe and sportspersonlike environment for all children.

INTERVENTIONS

May (2001) proposed a possible solution to what appears to be a disease of unsportspersonlike behavior in youth sport—cooperative games. He underscored, however, the challenges of initiating such a venture when children are inundated with contradictory messages and a societal reward structure that values "success through competition" (p. 388).

A possible venue for teaching moral education to youth is through the games component of physical education classes (PE), which should serve as a catalyst for the 'personal', 'social' and 'moral' development of children (socio-moral development, Theodoulides & Armour, 2001/02). As May (2001) suggested, the reciprocal relationships involved in team games has the potential of teaching children many of the social skills that fall under the rubric of sportspersonship (e.g., respecting others, not cheating, and task orientation). Theodoulides and Armour posed the following questions as a means of judging the accountability of PE in meeting social-moral goals, "What does PE offer which is more useful than other aspects of a modern curriculum where pupils often work together in groups and teams? What evidence do we have to support a special claim for effectiveness in this area? How far are we, and those outside the profession, relying upon historical claims for the role of team games in pupils' socio-moral development" (p. 9)? These questions have been examined through past research efforts; yet, with curriculum reform in PE, still are open to future examination. Historically, according to Theodoulides and Armour, there is little indication that PE has met the above needs (possibly due to games in PE being perceived as developing the physical side of youth and, depending on the culture, more competitive values). They made a case for further examination of what the goals of PE are with respect to 'personal', 'social' and 'moral' development. Indeed, attempts at curriculum reform (e.g., Ministry of Education Government of Quebec, 2001) have outlined the inclusion of these developmental elements within the PE curriculum. Nonetheless, a practical and oft-cited response of PE and other teachers has been "when and how can I implement it all"?

Stuart (2003) proposed that all individuals involved in youth sport be made aware of the moral issues surrounding youth sport. She suggested "enhancing moral sensitivity and moral intent.... " (p. 453) by developing programs that compel adults to examine their own beliefs and behavior (e.g., favoritism, special treatment of players, undue pressure). Guiverau and Duda (2002) also emphasized the importance of coaching education, particularly considering the wealth of findings that have demonstrated the effect of coaches on the development of the moral attitudes and behavior of their athletes. They recommended that through workshops and newsletters parents, sport organizers and others involved in youth sport be made aware of the factors that instill fair play. Indeed, the Internet has become a valuable source of information on sportspersonship. Federal, regional and community websites devoted to fair play have multiplied over the last view years. The challenge has become making all stakeholders aware of these resources.

Intervention work with children as young age 5 has been shown to improve levels of moral reasoning (Bredemeier, Weiss, Shields, & Cooper, 1986). As well, upper elementary children who participated in a fair play curriculum have been shown to develop more differentiated moral judgments and reasoning ability (Gibbons, Ebbeck, & Weiss, 1995). Both additional and long-term work has to be carried out before definitive conclusions can be made regarding in-school curricular and sport-based interventions. Interventions should be designed not only for youth, but also for coaches, parents, administrators, and officials. The main goal of intervention work should be to increase knowledge about issues of concern and to heighten awareness of one's personal values, beliefs, and behavior with the target goal being *change*. Perhaps research and practice in organizational change theory holds some answers.

Intervention research in school settings clearly has demonstrated that physical education alone is not necessarily the medium for the development of moral behavior. However, the inclusion of moral education within the physical education curriculum (e.g., using games with moral dilemmas) has lead to changes in attitudes and behavior with regard to fair play (Guivernau & Duda, 2002). Essentially, for the purpose of enhancing moral development, using environments that youth frequent would be a practical solution. To avoid controversy as to who decides what moral behavior is or is not, simply utilizing the basic definitions of fair play and sportsmanship introduced at the beginning of this chapter would be, at the very least, a good starting point.

There are numerous international sports bodies that have enumerated codes of ethics for youth sport. The Australian Sports Commission (Australian Sports Commission, n.d.) in particular has delineated a thorough list of components of fair play for players, parents, coaches, teachers, administrators and officials. Readers are referred to their website for details (www.ausport.gov.au/junior), however, examples from their code of ethics include, (a) for players: play by the rules, never argue with the referee, be a good sport; (b) for parents: encourage children to participate, do not force them; encourage children to play according to the rules and to settle disagreements without resorting to hostility or violence; respect officials' decisions and teach children to do likewise; respect the rights, dignity and worth of every young person; (c) for coaches: never ridicule or yell at a young player for making a mistake or not coming first, operate within the rules and spirit of your sport, avoid overplaying the talented players; (d) for teachers: create opportunities to teach appropriate sports behaviour; help young people understand the differences between junior competition and professional sport; help young people understand that playing by the rules is their responsibility; respect the rights, dignity and worth of every young person; (e) for administrators: involve young people in planning... and decision-making, provide quality supervision and instruction for junior players, help coaches and officials highlight appropriate behavior..., ensure that everyone involved... emphasizes fair play, rather than winning at all costs"; and (f) for officials: compliment and encourage all participants; be consistent, objective and courteous when making decisions; emphasize the spirit of the game... ; and be a good sport yourself. Actions speak louder than words. As a follow-up to providing each stakeholder with their respective code of ethics, a signed contract similar to those used by Athletes for a Better World (Athletes for a Better World, n.d.) in which the athlete, team members, coach and a parents become signatories would help reinforce a commitment to good sportspersonship (see http://www.abw.org/code.asp for examples of the respective contracts).

In conclusion, coaches, parents and other 'players' involved in youth sport can benefit from existing findings with regard to establishing a motivational climate that meets the needs and motivational orientation of young athletes. It is quite clear from the research that the specific motivational climate established by significant others influences young athletes' attitudes toward winning and fair play. In fact, research already has demonstrated that athletes not only personify the goal orientations exemplified by their coaches (Guivernau & Duda,

2002), but also that coaches' and players' own motivational orientations can be modified through intervention work (Boixados, Cruz, Torregrosa, & Valiente, 2004).

The underlying message of theories like Achievement Goal Theory is to instill in youth a sense of playing for fun, personal growth, socializing, increasing skill level and being an active participant—that is, setting up a task-oriented climate in sports. While individual qualities (dispositional factors) play an important role in how one perceives their success, coaches and others involved in the sport venue (e.g., umpires, parents) also can shape sport settings (situational factors) to strengthen more task-oriented values. It already has been demonstrated that when coaches emphasize a win or lose ethic, unsportspersonlike behavior, including cheating, ensues (Miller, Roberts, & Ommundsen, 2004). Unfortunately, creating an ethos of fair play in youth sport may be a challenge considering the 'dark side' of sport as depicted through the media and play at the elite and professional levels (the head-butting incident involving France's Zinedine Zidane at the 2006 World Cup of Soccer was a wonderful example as was Tonya Harding's attack on Nancy Kerrigan during the 1994 U.S. Figure Skating Championships). Even major international sporting events where the primary motivation is to win medals and better one's opponent do not always project the highest levels of sportspersonship. Concerns about fair play in the area of youth sport have put the challenge of dealing with it near the top of the youth sport agenda. The time has come to step up and meet this challenge through continued research, education, awareness and the communication of values of fair play through all media outlets.

REFERENCES

Athletes for a Better World. (no date). The code for living: Life principles learned through sports. Retrieved February 6, 2006, from http://www.abw.org/code.asp

Australian Sports Commission. (unknown). Junior sport: Codes of behavior. Retrieved February 6, 2006, from www.ausport.gov.au/junior

Australian Sports Commission. (unknown). Junior sport: Codes of behavior. Retrieved February 6, 2006, from www.ausport.gov.au/junior

Bandura, A. (1973). Aggression: A Social Learning Analysis. Englewood Cliffs, NJ: Prentice-Hall.

Bandura, A. (1986). Social foundations of thought and action. Englewood Cliffs, NJ: Prentice-Hall.

Boixados, M., Cruz, J., Torregrosa, M., & Valiente, L. (2004). Relationships among motivational climate, satisfaction, perceived ability, and fair play attitudes in young soccer players. Journal of Applied Sport Psychology, 16, 301-317.

Bredemeier, B. J. (1985). Moral reasoning and the perceived legitimacy of intentionally injurious sport acts. Journal of Sport Psychology, 7, 110-124.

Bredemeier, B. J., & Shields, D. L. (1986). Moral growth among athletes and nonathletes: a comparative analysis. Journal of Genetic Psychology, 147(1), 7-18.

Bredemeier, B. J., Weiss, M. R., Shields, D. L., & Cooper, D. (1986). The relationship of sport involvement with children's moral reasoning and aggression tendencies. Journal of Sport Psychology, 8, 304-318.

Bronfenbrenner, U. (2005). Making human beings human: Bioecological perspectives on human development. In U. Bronfenbrenner (Ed.), The bioecological theory of human development (pp. 3-21). Thousand Oaks, CA: Sage Publications, Inc.

Buford May, R. (2001). The sticky situation of sportsmanship: Contexts and contradictions in sportsmanship among high school boys' basketball players. Journal of Sport & Social Issues, 25(4), 372-389.

Canadian Centre for Ethics in Sport. (2002). 2002 Canadian public opinion survey on youth and sport: Final report. Ottawa, ON.

Chantal, Y., & Bernache-Assollant, I. (2003). A prospective analysis of self-determine sport motivation and sportspersonship orientations. Athletic Insight, 5(4), Retrieved January 27, 2006, from http://www.athleticinsight.com/Vol205Iss2004/Sportspersonship.htm.

Deci, E. L., & Ryan, R. M. (1985). Intrinsic motivation and self-determination in human behavior. New York: Plenum Press.

Duda, J. L., Olson, L. K., & Templin, T. J. (1991a). The relationship of task and ego orientation to sportsmanship attitudes and the perceived legitimacy of injurious acts. Research Quarterly for Exercise and Sport, 62, 297-334.

Duda, J. L., Olson, L. K., & Templin, T. J. (1991b). The relationship of task and ego orientation to sportsmanship attitudes and the perceived legitimacy of injurious acts. Research Quarterly for Exercise and Sport, 62, 297-334.

Gano-Overwaya, L. A., Guivernau, M., Magyar, T. M., Waldrond, J. J., & Ewing, M. E. (2005). Achievement goal perspectives, perceptions of the motivational climate, and sportspersonship: Individual and team effects. Psychology of Sport and Exercise, 6, 215-232.

Gibbons, S. L., Ebbeck, V., & Weiss, M. (1995). Fair play for kids: Effects on the moral development of children in physical education. Research Quarterly for Exercise and Sport, 66, 247-255.

Gilligan, C. (1982). In a different voice: Psychological theory and women's development. Cambridge, MA: Harvard University Press.

Guivernau, M., & Duda, J. L. (2002). Moral atmosphere and athletic aggressive tendencies in young soccer players. Journal of Moral Education, 31(1), 67-85.

Haan, N. (1991). Moral development and action from a social constructivist perspective. In W. Kurtines & J. Gewirtz (Eds.), Handbook of moral behavior and development, Vol. 1: Theory, (pp. 251-273). Hillsdale, N.J.: Lawrence Erlbaum Associates.

Kavussanu, M., & Roberts, G. C. (2001a). Moral functioning in sport: An achievement goal perspective. Journal of Sport and Exercise Psychology, 23, 37-54.

Kavussanu, M., & Roberts, G. C. (2001b). Moral functioning in sport: An achievement goal perspective. Journal of Sport and Exercise Psychology, 23, 37-54.

Kavussanu, M., Seal, A., & Philips, D. (in press). Observed prosocial and antisocial behaviors in male soccer teams: Age differences across adolescence and the role of motivational variables. Journal of Applied Sport Psychology.

Kohlberg, L. (1981). Essays on moral development: Vol. 1: The philosophy of moral development. San Francisco: Harper & Row.

Kohlberg, L. (1984). Essays on moral development: Vol. 2: The philosophy of moral development. San Francisco: Harper & Row.

Lemyre, P. N., Roberts, G., & Ommundsen, Y. (2002). Achievement goal orientations, perceived ability, and sportspersonship in youth soccer. Journal of Applied Sport Psychology, 14, 120-136.

May, R. A. B. (2001). The sticky situation of sportsmanship: Contexts and contradictions in sportsmanship among high school boys' basketball players. Journal of Sport & Social Issues, 25(4), 372-389.

Miller, B. W., Roberts, G. C., & Ommundsen, Y. (2004). Effect of motivational climate on sportspersonship among competitive youth male and female football players. Scandinavian Journal of Medicine & Science in Sports, 14(3), 193-202.

Miller, B. W., Roberts, G. C., & Ommundsen, Y. (2005). Effect of motivational climate on sportspersonship among competitive youth male and female football players. Scandinavian Journal of Medicine & Science in Sports, 14(3), 193-202.

Ministry of Education Government of Quebec. (2001). Quebec education program: Preschool and elementary education. Montreal, QC: Government of Quebec.

Murphy, S. (1999). The cheers and the tears: A healthy alternative to the dark side of youth sports today. San Francisco, CA: Jossey-Bass

Nicholls. (1989). The competitive ethos and democratic education. Cambridge, MA: Harvard University Press.

Ommundsen, Y., Roberts, G. C., Lemyre, P. N., & Treasure, D. (2003). Perceived motivational climate in male youth soccer: Relations to social-moral functioning, sportspersonship and team norm perceptions. Psychology of Sport and Exercise.

Peretti-Watel, P., Guagliardo, V., Verger, P., Pruvost, J., Mignon, P., & Obadia, Y. (2003). Sporting activity and drug use: alcohol, cigarette and cannabis use among elite student athletes. Addiction, 98(9), 1249-1256.

Proios, M., Doganis, G., & Athanailidis, I. (2004). Moral development and form of participation, type of sport, and sport experience. Perceptual and Motor Skills, 99(2), 633-642.

Roberts, G. C. (2001). Understanding the dynamics of motivation in physical activity: The influence of achievement goals, personal agency beliefs, and the motivational climate. In G. C. Roberts (Ed.), Advances in motivation in sport and exercise (pp. 1-50). Champaign, IL: Human Kinetics.

Shields, D. L., & Bredemeier, B. J. (1995). Character development and physical activity. Champaign, IL: Human Kinetics.

Shields, D. L., & Bredemeier, B. J. (2001). Moral development and behavior in sport. In R. Singer, H. Hausenblas & J. Christopher (Eds.), Handbook of sport psychology. New York: Wiley.

Shields, D. L., & Bredemeier, B. J. (unknown). Moral reasoning in the context of sport. Retrieved October 18, 2005, from http://tigger.ulc.edu/~Inucci/MoralEd/articles/shieldssport.html#top

Stephens, D. E., & Bredemeier, B. J. (1996). Moral atmosphere and judgments about aggression in girls' soccer: Relationships among moral and motivational variables. Journal of Sport and Exercise Psychology, 18, 158-173.

Stephens, D. E., & Kavanagh, B. (2003). Aggression in Canadian youth ice hockey: The role of moral atmosphere. International Sports Journal, 7(2), 109-119.

Stuart, M. (2003). Moral issues in sport: The child's perspective. Research Quarterly for Exercise and Sport, 74(4), 445-454.

Stuntz, C. P., & Weiss, M. (2003). Influence of social goal orientations and peer on unsportsmanlike play. Research Quarterly for Exercise and Sport, 74(4), 421-435.

Theodoulides, A., & Armour, K. M. (2001/02). Personal, social and moral development through team games: Some critical questions. European Physical Education Review, 7(1), 5-23.

Vallerand, R. J., & Losier, G. F. (1994). Self-determined motivation and sportsmanship orientations: An assessment of their temporal relationship. Journal of Sport and Exercise Psychology, 16, 229-245.

Vygotsky, L. S. (1962). Thought and Language. Cambridge, MA MIT Press.

Weiss, M., & Smith, A. L. (2002). Friendship quality in youth sport: Relationship to age, gender, and motivation variables. Journal of Sport & Exercise Psychology, 24, 420-437.

Wertsch, J. V. (1985). Cultural, Communication, and Cognition: Vygotskian Perspectives. Cambridge, UK: Cambridge University Press.

Chapter 3

ABUSE IN YOUTH SPORT

In my original proposal for this book, I had not intended to include the issue of abuse in youth sport. However, as more and more cases of abuse in sport surfaced in the media while doing the research for other chapters, I began to realize that this was unquestionably a contemporary issue, and one that had to be shared with individuals involved in youth sport. It is paradoxical, as proposed by Cense & Brackenridge (2001) that youth sport has been considered a venue for character development, and yet, more recently has been identified as a potential breeding ground for abuse cases. As suggested in *A Guide to Prevention and Awareness of Abuse for Youth Sports Associations* (*A guide to prevention and awareness of abuse for youth sports associations prepared by Bollinger, Inc.*, January 2005), qualities of sports participation such as close relationships with coaches who hold the 'power', out-of-town competitions, lack of reporting procedures and support systems for young athletes, and few witnesses to abusive acts increases the opportunities for abuse to take place.

In researching for this chapter, I unfortunately discovered that abuse in youth sport was an issue that for various reasons had been swept under the research rug until essentially the start of the new millennium. At this juncture, individual cases of child abuse of high profile, professional athletes started to surface in the media (e.g., the Sheldon Kennedy case in Canada or cases revolving around coaches Brett Sutton and Steve Woods in Australia, or, in 2006, the reported sexual assault of a 14-year old gymnast in Dallas for which the perpetrator was imprisoned for 15 years). I uncovered a number of theoretical pieces in my searches, but the research prior to 2000 was extremely sparse particularly in North America. In 2002, a special issue of *The Journal of Sexual Aggression* was published that focused on sexual abuse in sport. This special issue stemmed from growing interest in the area (Hartill, 2005). Naturally, there have been and are complexities in carrying out research on this topic. A major complication has been that victims of abuse have hesitated in coming forward with their stories considering the personal and so very delicate nature of personal concerns connected to child abuse.

The goal of this chapter is to introduce not only theoretical perspectives related to abuse in youth sport, but also to examine the various methodologies used in researching the topic. Research related to abuse in youth sport is timely, yet limited. Hopefully, in writing this chapter I will help to uncover and share valuable insights from the studies that already have been carried out as well as increase knowledge of the potential of this new frontier for further investigation. In doing so, hopefully, increased awareness will help bring to an end what appears to have become a growing worry in the world of youth sport.

Major categories of abuse include sexual, emotional, physical abuse and neglect (Brackenridge, Bringer, & Bishopp, 2005). MacGregor (1998) pointed out that "harassment includes a broad range of behaviours, such as verbal and physical abuse while also including racial harassment, homophobia, abusive coaching/teaching practices, sexual harassment and abuse and other practices that threaten the health and safety of participants" (p. 1). She suggested that harassment and abuse are on a continuum from more innocuous to more serious behaviors. Essentially, abuse is any form of discrimination against an individual. For example, with regard to homophobia, in the spring of 2006, a university coach in the United States was reprimanded for discriminating against a lesbian athlete. This was considered a form of abuse/harassment. Interestingly, as MacGregor pointed out, the intent behind the behavior is not necessarily what makes it harassment in the legal sense. Rather, it is the impact of the abuser's actions on the victim that define the behavior as abusive. Generally, however, the focus has been on the behavior of the perpetrator.

MacGregor (1998) provided a list of examples of harassment from sports. They included, for example, intentional injury, excessive exercise as punishment, ridicule, pressure to excel, intimidation (including physical), hazing, humiliation, and sexual innuendo. As she has so figuratively stated in suggested that there are positive ways of motivating athletes besides using abusive strategies, "... hockey players can play the game without having to put a marshmallow up their anus" (p. 3).

With more pressure on children to achieve success and possibly follow a professional path in their chosen sport and with the competitive nature of sport, elite child athletes are reported to be spending more and more time with coaches in order to reach the pinnacle of success. In fact, coaches have often replaced parents as having a significant influence in these children's lives so much so that the potential for coaches to take advantage of these relationships through abusive forms has become a major concern. The time and extreme dedication that young elite athletes give their sport in order to perform at the highest levels often isolates them from 'normal' childhood activities, and encourages a coach-athlete bond that places the adult in a powerful position as both parties work hard to fulfill mutual goals and aspirations (Gervis & Dunn, 2004). In this drive towards excellence, misuse of power by some coaches (and parents) has led to maltreatment of young athletes. This exploitation has surfaced through both sexual and non-sexual means. The issue has become of greater concern as stories of rape, sexual harassment in other forms, and emotional haranguing of young athletes has surfaced through the various media. Gervis and Dunn referred to Joan Ryan's 'must-read' book *Little Girls in Pretty Boxes* in which the latter provided examples of abuse in the worlds of figure skating and gymnastics. Interpreting Ryan's accounts, Gervis and Dunn maintained, "coaches were committing a legalized form of child abuse, which is hidden behind success" (p. 216). In other words, the means to success do not justify the end. However, winning at all costs may be the only reward that coaches, parents and young athletes have been responsive to in pursuit of that Olympic gold medal! Selective attention to performance and success can blind those very individuals with a direct interest in a young athlete's achievements to harmful incidents along the path to glory. Sadly, as Gervis and Dunn implied, certain abusive coaching styles have been accepted as the norm. This view has been supported by MacGregor (1998) who suggested that despite limited amount of research and small sample sizes, it has been estimated that approximately 40 to 50 per cent of athletes have experienced anything from slight harassment to severe abuse.

SEXUAL HARASSMENT

Sexual abuse or harassment comes in many forms. In the United States, "the legal definition of sexual molestation is an act of a person who forces, coerces or threatens another person to have any form of sexual contact or to engage in any type of sexual activity" (*A guide to prevention and awareness of abuse for youth sports associations prepared by Bollinger, Inc.*, January 2005, p. 6). It can include sexual innuendo or more overt sexual advances such as touching, showing or using a child in pornography.

There appear to be varying theories about the roots of sexual harassment. Thomas (as cited in Fasting, Brackenridge, & Sundgot-Borgen, 2004) explained that psychologists primarily have focused on the abuser's motivations and emotions while sociologists have suggested that sexual harassment is an extension of society's "asymmetrical power relations between men and women" (p. 383). Thomas' position, as explained by Fasting, Brackenridge, and Sundgot-Borgen, has been that combinations of both psychological and sociological factors play a role. This interactionist position, as well as possible biological origins, seems reasonable.

Cense and Brackenridge (2001) cited Finkelhor's four-factor theory of sexual abuse, which has roots in sociological theory, and had remained untested within sport research. According to Finkelhor, sexual abuse occurs if the following four factors occur in sequence: (1) motivation of abuser to sexually abuse, (2) weakening of internal and external (3) inhibitions of the abuser, and (4) the abuser's prevailing over the child-victim. A sound theory of sexual abuse in sport (in fact, all abuse) should include both person- and situation-specific factors. Throughout their work, Brackenridge and her colleagues (as cited in Cense & Brackenridge, 2001) made an attempt at delineating those risk factors related to coach (e.g., sex, age, reputation, record of sexual crimes, trust of parents, use of car), athlete (e.g., sex, age, size, self-esteem, relationship with parents, knowledge of sexual harassment issues), and sport (e.g., individual/team, location of competitions, dress requirements, code of ethics or not, trips away). Some of these factors have been, are, and should be the focus of research. Cense and Brackenridge proposed taking a developmental approach to studying the most sensitive periods for sexual abuse to occur. They cited work by Brackenridge's research group in which it had been proposed that an athlete's reaching a level of international competition appeared to be a critical period ("stage of imminent achievement or SIA", p. 64). This theory has yet to be confirmed. As evinced from the research described below, theories exist attempting to link type of sport and incidence of sexual abuse. Research of this nature has been driven by researchers' need to identify specific risk factors that may lead abuse so that potential abuse can be stopped in its tracks.

OTHER FORMS OF ABUSE

Gervis and Dunn (2004) alluded to Doyle's definition of *emotional abuse* as "... acts (that) are committed by parent figures who are in a position of differential power that renders the child vulnerable. Such acts damage immediately or ultimately the behavioural, cognitive, affective, social and psychological functioning of the child" (p. 217).

Like sexual harassment, misuse of power and the vulnerability of children have surfaced as critical elements of most abusive relationships. In fact, as MacGregor (1998) suggested, power has been the root of most abuse cases. This power has surfaced as "reward power, traditional power, charismatic power, expert power, coercive power, and social power... some form of conjugal right" (Burke, 2001, p. 229-230). An imbalance of power is fine (e.g., coach-athlete, teacher-student, parent-child) as long as the power is not used in damaging ways. Furthermore, abuse has been shown to encroach on a child's innermost psychological core making the latter more and more defenseless as they grow to be dependent on the only expert, the "parental figure" (Gervis & Dunn, 2004, p. 217) who can guide them to success.

Physical abuse is often easier to recognize as the child may experience bruising from being kicked, hit or punched. *Neglect* in sport is common as coaches leave athletes sitting on the bench, ignore young participants' needs, or do not provide young athletes with as safe an environment for play as possible. Zero-tolerance should be the norm for anyone who abuses a child in any form in the disguise of discipline.

CHILD PROTECTION

Growing awareness of child abuse in society at large has led to heightened consciousness of abuse in youth sport. The existence of child abuse in sport in addition to the revelations from high-profile cases from the sports world, has led to the development of child protection (CP) policies. Brackenridge and her colleagues have pointed out that the development of CP policies in sport in England was slow in coming due to embarrassment, denial and concern over losing participants. However, various sport bodies in England have more recently adopted CP practices promoted by the Child Protection in Sport Unit (CPSU, www.thecpsu.org.uk). The latter developed national standards for the protection of youth in sport to which funding has been tied since 2001(Brackenridge, Bringer, & Bishopp, 2005). CP policies have to be both in place and evaluated.

While the focus has been primarily on child sexual abuse (CSA), CP policies are designed to identify and handle all kinds of abuse—sexual, emotional, and physical (Brackenridge, Bringer, & Bishopp, 2005). Brackenridge, Bringer and Bishopp delineated a four-point model of CP policies and procedures. The model includes *protection through referral* of an athlete subjected to abuse, *protection through leadership* (promoting 'good practice' in interaction with athletes--a concern of parents), *protection against false accusations* (a concern of coaches), and *protection of the sport* (a concern of administrators). Unfortunately, since the issue of child protection (CP) in sport is a relatively new concept, adequate measures of the effects of CP interventions have been scarce. Research in the field is still in its infancy stage.

Canada (e.g., Canadian Association for the Advancement of Women and Sport and the Canadian Center for Ethics in Sport), Australia (e.g., Australian Sports Commission), the United States (e.g., National Council of Youth Sports), and the U.K. (Child Protection in Sport Unit) have established institutions whose goals are to develop awareness of, educate and design policies to protect children (Brackenridge, Bringer, & Bishopp, 2005). Readers are urged to view the respective websites and links for research-related and a wealth of practical guidelines as well as general information for parents, coaches, and athletes. As Brackenridge et al. reported, these federal initiatives serve as umbrella organizations. In the past, individual sport bodies carried out their own CP programs.

For example, in England, the Football Association (FA) was one of the primary sports bodies to be concerned with child abuse. Components of the FA's CP policy include:

"Key principles:
- The child's welfare is paramount.
- All children have a right to be protected from abuse regardless of their age, gender, disability, culture language racial origin, religious beliefs or sexual identity.
- All suspicions and allegations of abuse will be taken seriously and responded to swiftly and appropriately.

Aims:
- To develop a positive pro-active policy to protect all children and young people, who play or participate in football, enabling them to do so in an enjoyable and safe environment.
- To deliver quality assured Child Protection Training and build a network of accredited Child Protection tutors to facilitate this delivery, supported (where appropriate) by the National Coaching Foundation (NCF).
- To demonstrate best practice in Child Protection.
- To promote ethics and high standards in football" (Brackenridge, Bringer, & Bishopp, 2005, p. 32).

The above principles are far-reaching, and undoubtedly a model that can be adopted and adapted across different sport bodies or individual teams.

The FA commissioned the National Society for the Prevention of Cruelty to Children (NSPCC) to conduct research on child protection within its sport (project Goal, Brackenridge et al., 2005). An evaluation of the value of the CP intervention in the FA was reported in Brackenridge et al. (2004). Briefly, Brackenridge and her colleagues in the UK used models of 'activation states' to examine longitudinally changes in knowledge, emotions, behavior and dialogue related to the football culture in England (soccer in North American) since the introduction of the CP policies. The underlying model for their research program was borrowed from, for example, the schools of health psychology, management and organizational sociology. They examined cultural change within the organization with analyses at varying points in time. As Brackenridge et al. (2005) pointed out, accepting change by members of an organization can be a complex process across all manner of institutions, and establishing a CP policy for the FA was a form of change in which the various 'change agents' had to acknowledge the benefits of the program. The researchers evaluated what they called "unreactive, active, proactive, or opposed (reactions)... to indicate the level of activation of each stakeholder group towards CP in football" (Brackenridge et al., 2005, p. 9). These states were then linked to what people said (their own 'voices), their behavior ('action'), feelings and knowledge regarding the intervention. For example, was what an individual said about the CP program illustrative of negative or positive feelings? Was their reaction indicative of increased awareness of CP? Charting individual profiles of activation states on a matrix allowed the researchers to "provide a picture of change" (p. 15) in all stakeholders' feelings, reactions, knowledge, and words over time, and informed the researchers as to whether actions and words (for example) were in synchrony. The methodology used in the model of activation states has proven to be effective in evaluating acceptance or conflict with new programs like the CP initiative. The specifics of the study are described under the 'research' section that follows.

RESEARCH

As already mentioned, research on sexual harassment in non-sport venues like work and educational environments has been considered rather recent (Fasting, Brackenridge, & Sundgot-Borgen, 2004). Much of the research that has been carried out has taken a more sociological approach as questions related to the links between an environment's being male- or female- dominated and the incidence of sexual harassment have been explored. One position has been that under-representation by women in positions of authority may have been cause for more incidents of sexual harassment (Fasting, Brackenridge, & Sundgot-Borgen). The prevailing view, particularly by feminist scholars, has been that because sport generally has been male-dominated in terms of both the hierarchy of 'actors' and values, there are increased opportunities for sexual harassment to occur. There are others who have felt that the plight of abused male athletes has been overlooked, and they have challenged the 'male perpetrator-female victim' archetype and under-representation in research of males as victims and females as perpetrators (e.g., Hartill, 2005). The focal concern should be the safety of *all* children involved in youth sport—male or female! There is a considerable shortage of research (and awareness for that matter) on abuse in youth sport regardless of gender-related philosophies.

Much of the reported research has been carried out in the UK (e.g., Brackenridge, Bringer, & Bishopp, 2005; Brackenridge et al., 2005; Hartill, 2005). Albeit limited, research that exists on abuse in sport has been qualitative, quantitative or a combination of the two. Unfortunately, as pointed out by Fasting, Brackenridge, and Sundgot-Borgen (2004), many of the studies that have been carried out have not been without problems such as sample size, non-response, and inconsistency in methodologies thereby limiting the ability to establish valid and reliable overall trends. Referred to earlier in the chapter, Brackenridge, Bringer, and Bishopp (2005) identified the Football Association (FA) in the UK as the first sports body in that country to commission research on child protection including investigating whether CP programs were already in place within the sport and the nature of these programs, attitudes about ongoing programs, program goals, and the impact of the policies on football. The research was designed over a period of five years, and involved a two-part plan including both qualitative (current facts regarding CP policies and follow-up) and quantitative (assessment of current attitudes of all stakeholders, and changes in beliefs) measures. The results of the research are documented in a number of manuscripts published by Brackenridge and her colleagues (e.g., Brackenridge, Bringer, & Bishopp, 2005; Brackenridge et al., 2004; Fasting, Brackenridge, & Sundgot-Borgen, 2004).

In the UK, many of the reported cases of abuse have been put into a database for the use of researchers interested in the various factors related to abuse in sport. Brackenridge's research team has used this database extensively to examine such variables as age, gender and risk factors (e.g., Brackenridge, Bringer, & Bishopp, 2005). Other factors gleaned through the database have included, nature and severity of abuse, demographics of abusers and victims, whether and how cases are settled, and far-reaching 'lessons' from the cases (Brackenridge, Bringer, & Bishopp). Identifying risk factors for abuse through this database also had led to the design and evaluation of various CP interventions.

In their most recent report, Brackenridge, Bringer, and Bishopp (2005) described in detail the extensive results of their research initiative with major participants in the FA. Their report included information from children, parents, coaches, CP officers, and administrators. Their preliminary first year audit revealed that most of the young athletes were unaware of the FA's attempts to protect their interests. In fact, a surprising number of negative experiences were reported. For example, 41% reported verbal bullying, 40% swearing at coaches or referees and officials, and 23% physical bullying. Eighty-two percent of parents were satisfied with the treatment of youth in the FA while 59% felt the FA handled child protection issues very well or quite well. Similar to the athletes, most parents (89.7%) were unaware of the FA's child protection initiatives (i.e., the *Goal* campaign). The researchers concluded that parents were the least informed group with regards to CP as were referees (86.1%). Coaches, managers and teachers were supportive and generally interested in practical information. Coaches reported being intolerant towards bullying by athletes and parents. However, they also held many misconceptions about what constitutes child abuse and best practice. Despite the generally positive attitudes of coaches, managers and teachers toward CP policies and the intervention work itself, some coaches commented that their counterparts did not always practice on the field what they preached at the workshops. Finally, some participants expressed attitudes that those involved in the sport at the professional level should become more involved in CP efforts by serving as positive role models. Overall, there was general consensus that efforts made by the FA were proactive and valuable with respect to child safety in sport despite the disturbing finding that the those higher in authority were the least well-versed and committed to CP measures. Suggested priorities for dealing with abuse included introducing criminal background checks, strategies for false accusations, and "high personal standards of child protection and welfare" (Brackenridge, Bringer, & Bishopp, p. 44).

Fasting, Brackenridge, and Sundgot-Borgen (2004) explored those risk factors associated with abuse in sport by also examining whether they differed across 56 different sports. Their rationale was that if risk factors could be identified, interventions could be designed and implemented. Despite the added concern that those involved in CP projects might suffer from "welfare overload" (Brackenridge, Bringer, & Bishopp, 2005, p. 44), the claim was also made that results of studies in this area and their practical implications could have political undertones for individual sports. In other words, research designed to tease out risk factors could be likened to a two-sided coin. As Fasting, Brackenridge, and Sundgot-Borgen mentioned, if a specific sport was targeted as fueling more abuse than other sports, this could cause a ripple effect with parents denying their child's participating in that sport. This has happened in the UK where a case of sexual abuse in a particular sport was uncovered, and garnered notoriety within the larger society. Identifying sports as risky or not has resulted in both "false positives and false negatives" (Fasting, Brackenridge, & Sundgot-Borgen, p. 2) with the possibility of some sports being unjustly targeted while others remain ignored. The goal of their research was to more clearly define the risks factors of sexual abuse in sport in order to avoid such errors of omission and commission. As reinforced in discussing the various topics throughout this book, both situation- and person-related factors must be considered when investigating the mechanisms of abuse in youth sport. I propose that approaches must be both ecological and interactionist.

More specifically, participants in Fasting, Brackenridge, and Sundgot-Borgen's study (2004) were 553 elite, female athletes (ages 15 - 39) from 56 different sports. Rather than studying and therefore targeting the sport genre themselves, the researchers used the following classification system to group the sports, and to identify those classifications more open to harassment: *formation* (individual or group), *clothing* (little to a lot), *gender structure* (including neutral) and *gender culture* (including neutral). As part of a larger study conducted in Norway, the athletes either completed a survey, or were interviewed by telephone as to whether they had ever been subjected to sexual harassment/abuse, and if so, reported the severity and by whom (e.g., male or female, authority figure or fellow player). An 11-item instrument was designed based on Brackenridge's characterization of sexual harassment and abuse (Brackenridge as cited in Fasting, Brackenridge, & Sundgot-Borgen, 2004). Examples of items included, "repeated unwanted sexual remarks concerning one's body, private life, sexual orientation, (and) severe sexual abuse defined as attempted rape or rape" (Fasting et al., p. 378). Fasting, Brackenridge, and Sundgot-Borgen concluded that sexual harassment was not endemic to any particular sport. In point of fact, they discovered that it was present in every sport grouping. Although not significant, the incidence of sexual harassment was higher in individual over team sports, and was instigated more often than not from individuals outside of the sport setting. Amount of clothing worn was not linked significantly to sexual harassment. On the contrary, the more a uniform covered an athlete, the more reported incidents! Gender-related effects also were reported. Although results revealed that the incidence of sexual harassment in male-dominated organizations did not appear to be a significant factor, those female athletes who participated in traditionally male sports had experienced significantly more sexual harassment than athletes in other sports. It was reported that the abuse originated from their peers more than from authority figures. As a possible explanation, Fasting, Brackenridge, and Sundgot-Borgen suggested that male athletes hold "patriarchal power" (p. 383) over women entering *'their'* sports. The women were characterized as "intruding into" (p. 384) traditionally 'male' sports. The origins of this interpretation are founded in the feminist view that sport has always been considered a masculine entity into which women have encroached. Fasting, Brackenridge, and Sundgot-Borgen's conclusion that sport participation rather than sport type instigates sexual harassment was revealing, and is worthy of further investigation.

In an earlier study, Cense & Brackenridge (2001) carried out work in the Netherlands the purpose of which also was to identify risk factors for sexual harassment and abuse among 14 athletes (eleven females, three males) who had been sexually abused. Purposive sampling (often used in qualitative research) was used to choose the participants. Eight athletes had been abused before age 16 while the remainder as adults. In all cases, males were the perpetrators. Six had played sports at the recreational level while the others participated at the elite level. Sport type varied. Personal accounts of sexual abuse were collected through semi-structured interviews. Emergent themes were identified from interview transcripts, and comparisons between the pre-16-year-olds and adults were explored. One goal of their study was to establish an identifiable developmental progression of abuse, or temporal stages, using Finkelhor's four factor model of sexual abuse and risk factors for sexual abuse in sport as previously identified by Brackenridge and her colleagues in previous work. In reporting their results, Cense and Brackenridge focused on information gathered from the younger athletes' experiences. Using Finkelhor and Brackenridge's work as a template, the temporal model they tested included *stages* of abuse (e.g., motivation of perpetrator, selecting a victim, actual abuse and harassment after abuse), *components* of the abuse (e.g., emotional need of perpetrator, sexual arousal, opportunities and relationship between athlete and perpetrator) and *indicators* of abuse (e.g., need to feel powerful and in control, little bound by ethical codes, massage, and need for confirmation and attention by the athlete). With results in hand, heightened and early awareness of the risk factors could be the focal point of developing proactive prevention policies and subsequent interventions.

The abusers in their study were described as 'intimate paedophiles' as opposed to 'aggressive' or 'criminal opportunist' as they "gradually entrapped" (Cense & Brackenridge, 2001, p. 67) their victims. In fact, sadly, their targets reported having felt somewhat special in being singled out (special in a positive way). Moreover, feelings of belongingness nicely fed into and meshed with the victims' need for relatedness. For example, one athlete was reported as saying "I was drawn more and more towards the coach, as he was the one who was there for me. Of course, it's fantastic to have someone who empathizes with you" (Cense & Brackenridge, p. 68). Similar perpetrator-victim relationships have been reported in the general research on sexual abuse. This bond has been depicted as coaches' overstepping normal boundaries of power and control by manipulating victims and taking advantage of their weaknesses (Cense & Brackenridge).

Other central factors identified in the model included the age differential between the perpetrator and victim (related to social norms regarding the 'power' adults have over younger individuals). Cense and Brackenridge (2001) referred to this phenomenon as "structural power" (p. 68). They proposed that both dysfunctional relationships with parents and general ignorance of the elements of sexual abuse (a good place to start in the education of young athletes!) sets up these athletes for perpetrators' perverted intrusions into their lives. Cense and Brackenridge learned that out-of-town tournaments, massages by the coach, visits to the coach's home or being chauffeured by the coach provided particular opportunities for abuse. Results also portrayed athletes as generally unaware or in denial about the abuse as it occurred, or generally feeling helpless. Some reported not realizing they were abused until they were older. In fact, half of them experienced the abuse for several years without mentioning the experience to others. Again, these are symptoms common to abuse victims and not particular to the world of sport. The hierarchy of power and the want to achieve particular goals in their sport put the athletes into a vulnerable position that some could not break away from—some did not recognize the signs, some did not have the skills to disengage, and some felt special. Cense and Brackenridge reported various ways that the athletes left their sport (if they did)—quit, developed eating disorders, lost interest in their sport, or developed other close relationships. Ages 16 to 18 were seen as a critical period when athletes broke away. This phase corresponds to athletes' becoming more autonomous and searching for other venues of personal interest. According to Cense and Brackenridge, a coach's losing their sexual grip on an athlete sometimes led to other forms of harassment particularly if the latter continued playing. Abuse was reported to have resulted in such symptoms as severe emotional problems, reductions in self-confidence, disruptions in 'normal' adolescent development including developing healthy social relationships, and quitting the sport—"the after-effects influence the rest of your life. It has taken away a part of my youth" (Brackenridge as cited in Cense & Brackenridge, p. 71).

Gervis and Dunn (2004) also carried out a retrospective investigation. They examined coaches' emotional abuse of elite young athletes (ages 8 – 16). Using purposive chain sampling, they found twelve participants identified as elite athletes who, as children, had performed at that level for an average of 8 years. Men coached half the females (N = 4) and 75% of the males (N = 3). Using semi-structured interviews, the participants were asked to reflect on their experiences across a variety of sports. Gervis and Dunn used Barbarino et al.'s. (as cited in Gervis and Dunn) eight-point code of behaviors in classifying the responses of these former elite youth athletes into categories of emotional abuse. The athletes' emotional responses to the abuse and perceptions of the intensity of the behavior were also critical in defining whether the behavior fit into the 'abuse' schema. Results from the interviews uncovered the following frequency of reported behaviors: belittling and shouting (100%), threats (75%), humiliation (75%), scapegoating (58%), rejection or snubs (50%), and feelings of isolation (33%). The participants also reported experiencing a lower sense of self worth, feelings of stupidity, depression, fear and anger amongst other symptoms which often lingered well past the episodes of abuse ("... the pain of that I think I'll always remember", Gervis & Dunn, p. 221). Interestingly, they uncovered that coaches' negativity correlated with athletes' advancement up the ladder toward more elite levels in their sport, and as long as athletes were successful, abusive behavior had become the accepted norm for coaches ("Yes, he just became some power maniac because I was good; he thought that it was all his doing", Gervis & Dunn, p. 221). The data on the effects of gender of coach or athlete was not reported. Such a breakdown would have been informative considering that the conventional paradigm has been one of male perpetrator-female victim yet the numbers were too small to make comparisons. The athletes essentially viewed themselves as being caught in a 'Catch 22' --dependent on their coach in the pursuit of excellence in their sport. Of note, Gervis and Dunn also reported that the participants found the interviews somewhat cathartic. This finding in and of itself speaks for the need for support networks for athletes. At the very least, young athletes should have someone or some organized body to turn to for help. Indeed, considering some of the trends, more research is warranted using larger samples and more robust designs and statistical procedures combining both qualitative and quantitative methods. Gervis and Dunn did demonstrate, however, that the methodology for investigating abuse in familial situations can be applied to the sports milieu.

WHO IS A PERPETRATOR?

Research has shown that 70% - 89% of sexual abusers were abused themselves and that the majority are males (Ryan as cited in Fried, 1996). A publication by Lanning for The Center for Missing and Exploited Children has delineated those qualities inherent to child molesters as well as the myths surrounding the perpetrators (as cited in, *A guide to prevention and awareness of abuse for youth sports associations prepared by Bollinger, Inc.*, January 2005). Characteristics include:

- "Sexually abused as a child
- Limited social contact as teenagers
- Premature separation/discharge from the military
- Prior arrests or convictions for abuse or related offenses
- History of frequent or unexpected moves
- Over 25, single, never married
- Lives alone or with parents
- If married, may be a marriage of convenience
- Excessive interest in children; idealizes children
- Seeks legitimate access to children
- Has limited peer relationships
- Has specific age and gender preferences; associates and friends are young
- Skilled at identifying vulnerable victims and giving them the attention they seek
- Seduces with attention, affection and gifts
- Skilled at manipulating children, lowering their inhibitions and increasing the likelihood that they will cooperate" (*A guide to prevention and awareness of abuse for youth sports associations prepared by Bollinger, Inc.*, p. 9).

Abusers do not satisfy most commonly held stereotypes (*A guide to prevention and awareness of abuse for youth sports associations prepared by Bollinger, Inc.*, January 2005). For this reason, they are not easy to identify. They are *not* necessarily 'dirty old men' (some are pillars of their communities), of low intelligence, addicted to drugs and/or alcohol, sexually frustrated or homosexual, or strangers to their victims. In fact, as mentioned in "Passing the Trash" (2002), 'acquaintance abusers' commit approximately 40% of sexual abuse acts and a larger percentage against boys. The Lanning report has been a valuable resource for a variety of sports including rowing and lacrosse. With caution, coaches and parents can use these signals to identify possible perpetrators.

Trocme and Schumaker (1999) uncovered similar characteristics in school and recreational settings. Analyzing the data from the Ontario Incidence Study, they revealed that family members (e.g., parents, siblings, relatives) accounted for 78% of sexual abuse cases, friends and other acquaintances 20% of the cases, while others, including day care educators and recreational staff, 2.6%. Trocme and Schumaker warned that making inferences from studies that are carried out by police or child welfare groups can present a skewed picture of abusers as only reported cases are examined. In point of fact, they pointed out that a substantial number of cases remain unreported, and suggested that "sexual abuse of children in educational and recreational settings represent a serious problem in Canada" (p.629).

Nack and Yaeger (1998) classified types of abusers using categories provided by the FBI. Pedophiles were described as either, (1) *situational* child abusers (opportunistic) and (2) *preferential* child abusers (actively seeks out children for sex—introverted and seducer). The introverted abuser lacks the social skills to charm children. She/he either engages very young child under duress, and/or stalks, makes obscene phone calls, exposes themselves or contacts children through Internet chat rooms. The seducer, on the other hand, relying on their engaging personality, gains easy access to children by seeking employment where they can best 'hunt'—working in such milieus as schools, youth sport clubs, summer camps, etc. Because of their outgoing personality this type of molester is both able to win over parents and gain access to a child's emotional weaknesses. The seducer goes from location to location avoiding detection, or shifting locale when they themselves feel pursued. Because there have been so few documented cases of abuse in youth sport, statistics are difficult to find. An article in The Economist ("Passing the Trash," 2002) reported that in only 1% of the cases did a school district superintendent attempt to revoke a culprit's teaching license. In the educational sector, such negligence is so common that educators have referred to this phenomenon as 'passing the trash' ("Passing the Trash," 2002).

Abusers tend to be singularly successful manipulators who manage to contest and manipulate reality (e.g., "no, I am not like that anymore"). Illustrative of this, Nack and Yaeger (1998) described the behavior of one particular "beloved and winning" (p.2) coach who was well-respected in his community. Norman Watson had coached Little League baseball for over 25 years, and his teams were highly successful. He had been confined to two mental hospitals for committing acts of child molestation. After five years of treatment, and despite being on probation, he embarked on a new coaching career in another location during the 1990s. Parents had perceived Watson as being personable, beloved, glib, engaging and gifted. Most importantly, the parents valued his winning record. However, Watson's past was about to catch up with him. After 23 years of silence, one of his previous victims decided to hire a private detective to see what had happened to the man who had molested him. With the investigation, rumours started spreading in Watson's new community, and a couple whose child was on Watson's team verified through a sex offender registry that he was in fact listed. On confronting Watson, the Little League Board of Directors accepted his lies of having reformed. Ironically, the couple that had raised the issue was expelled from the Board while Watson continued both coaching and molesting! The inquiries and discovery of his past criminal record set the stage for Watson's final downfall however. In the midst of accusations and counter accusations on the Little League Board, children who had been molested by Watson finally came forward. He was finally arrested, charged and convicted to 84 years imprisonment having confessed to spending most of his life sexually abusing by his own account "a couple of hundred" (Nack & Yaeger, p. 1) children.

The above scenario underscores the illusive personality of most abusers in youth sport (for more youth sport-related examples, see Fried, 1996). They are manipulative, lying and adept at avoiding the consequences of what they do. As mentioned, parents are often blinded by their friendly and ingratiating personality, and ignore warning signs. Research has supported the fact that abusers open their arms to their victims, and play on the latter's neediness. Fried reported that a child's appearance can be a sign of weakness to the abuser (e.g., uncombed hair, dirty clothes, and a generally unkempt look). One quality that characterizes abusers is the extensive amount of time they very calculatingly spend with their victims outside of the sporting venue (Zaichkowsky, 2000). Zaichowsky also reported that abusers tend to target children where parents have split up. The victims remain silent as they often are fearful of being stigmatized by the label of homosexual, of not making the team, or of being denied recommendations for scholarships to institutions of higher education (Zaichowsky, Nack & Yaeger). As the research has revealed, victims have been described as usually conflicted. They enjoy the attention and emotional connection with the molester, but are uneasy in relation to the physical abuse ("I was embarrassed about it and I am still embarrassed about it", Nack & Yaeger, 1998, p. 5). At the same time, however, they are afraid of the judgments by the outside world, and often do not have the skills to disentangle themselves from the 'sticky web'.

VICTIMS

What are possible signs that a child has been or is being abused? According to Cense and Brackenridge (2001), missing practices, losing interest in the sport, performing below their ability, becoming withdrawn (or out of character) or ill may be indicative of being involved in an abusive relationship. One could append the following warning signs from the Bollinger report (*A guide to prevention and awareness of abuse for youth sports associations prepared by Bollinger, Inc.*, January 2005): signs of physical abuse, mood swings and heightened anxiety, poor peer relations, nightmares, drug or alcohol use, and problems with authority. Brackenridge (1996) listed the following cognitive warning signs that might result from abuse: "lack of concentration; inability to make decisions, prioritize, focus on tasks; memory problems; loss of perspective; placing one's needs as a low priority" (p. 14). Negative self talk also could be included on the list.

Victims have been shown to come from dysfunctional families, and tend to be social isolates (Cense & Brackenridge, 2001). As MacGregor (1998) suggested, victims of abuse are from all age groups and gender. She identified aboriginal and disabled athletes as well as social isolates and those without good support networks as more at risk for abuse. Because victims often are showered with gifts and given special privileges by their abusers, they habitually do not report abusive acts out of their own shame and guilt. It has been reported that children feel comfortable enough to share stories with their peers so caring adults should be ready to act on any rumours ("Passing the Trash," 2002).

Vulnerability to abuse has generally been found in the smaller, younger, more shy, less assertive, more dependent, female, emotionally challenged, racially distinct, and elite populations as well as in those athletes feeling pressure to excel (Brackenridge, 1996). Victims tend to be poor communicators. Essentially, these vulnerabilities place these child-athletes into powerless positions with respect to those in authority. In addition to being aware of some of the characteristics of abusers, concerned adults also should become aware of and respond to cues inherent to victims. Policies must be drawn up to protect these vulnerable athletes at all levels of youth sport. Needless to say, interventions ought to be designed to educate and empower these youngsters, and evidence-based research is needed to evaluate the effectiveness of these programs.

INTERVENTION AND PREVENTION

As already highlighted, data have illustrated that repeat offences are common despite the perpetrators of abuse having been incarcerated (Gibbons et al. as cited in Cense & Brackenridge, 2001). Reconviction rates run as high as 10 to 29 percent with girls and 13 to 40 percent with boys. The question that needs to be addressed is how to keep these manipulative abusers away from those venues that allow them to commit abusive acts. It is not an easy task, however, as abusers move from place to place re-establishing new relationships with unaware youth, their parents and administrators as the Norman Watson case has illustrated. Cense and Brackenridge have recommended that the boundaries between coach and athlete must be clearly delineated through an explicit code of conduct. Educational programs (awareness training, Brackenridge, 1996) targeted to all stakeholders involved in youth sports should clarify to participants what constitutes appropriate behavior. The conundrum, as Cense and Brackenridge have warned, has been that these codes and educational programs have been of little interest to offenders whose perceived power over their athletes has gone unquestioned. Through well-designed educational interventions, athletes as well as their parents could become more attuned to the risk factors and signs characteristic of dysfunctional and possibly abusive relationships—"... coach gradually shifted limits, building up a strong bond of trust, giving extra attention, nagging, taking advantage of amorous feelings... influencing parents, setting team members against each other... " (Cense & Brackenridge, p. 71). Children must be safe! They must feel empowered to respond to overtures of abuse! No matter how young they are, youth sport participants should be included in discussions as to what the boundaries adults they come into contact with are in addition to being provided with well-organized and accessible support systems.

The benefits of participating in sport and physical activity outweigh a parents' removing the abused child from sport altogether (Trocme & Schumaker, 1999). A change in venue might be a better solution. In fact, Trocme and Shumaker cited examples of research indicating that participation in sport helped victims deal with the abuse and that sport and recreation could serve as a "protective factor against abuse" (p. 33). The vast majority of research findings related to the positive effects of physical activity on self-esteem, anxiety, feelings of belongingness, or depression, for example, would support such a claim.

MacGregor (1998) suggested that the following actions be taken should abuse rear its ugly head: 1) clearly delineate policies and procedures for defining, reporting and dealing with participants in the abusive situation while also identifying support personnel, 2) utilize rigorous recruitment and screening processes for prospective coaches including reference and/or police record checks (unfortunately, shown to be of limited value), interviews, supervision and evaluation, 3) establish clear boundaries as to what is suitable and undesirable behavior for those in positions of power including both verbal and nonverbal behavior, 4) institute *change* within a sporting body or team that commits to incorporating the above proactive elements. Obviously, a zero-tolerance policy toward abuse and abusers must be implemented at all levels of youth sport. Readers are encouraged to read MacGregor's article for an invaluable 24–step intervention program and timeline for preventing and dealing with harassment and abuse some of the elements of which are mentioned above. As well, stakeholders within youth sport are encouraged to adopt or adapt the very valuable forms supplied in the Bollinger report (*A guide to prevention and awareness of abuse for youth sports associations prepared by Bollinger, Inc.*, January 2005)—*Employee/Volunteer Affidavit, Employee/Volunteer Application*, and *Zero-Tolerance Policy Against Abuse*. These documents formalize permission to carry out criminal background checks, to request references and work records, and to clearly delineate the boundaries, procedures and required behaviors for prevention of abusive acts towards children. It has been recommended not only that parents instill in their children the need to report

MacGregor (1998) has provided some useful "prevention tips" (p. 7) for parents. For example:

- Do not put coaches on a pedestal because of their record of success.
- Empower your child with knowledge of what constitutes abuse and how to respond to it.
- Attend practices and games and be wary of practices that are not open to parents.
- Be suspicious of presents from coaches and an inordinate amount of time that the coach spends with your child.
- Report any incidents of abuse that your child shares with you. Insure that your child feels safe and secure enough to inform you of such occurrences and provide counseling for the child.
- Become cognizant of changes in your child's behavior or mood. Symptoms may include various disorders (sleep, depression), declining grades, vomiting, lesions, and asocial behavior.
- Communicate with your child! Discuss sexuality and when innocent teasing becomes more intrusive harassment and abuse.
- Model appropriate behavior in the home.

Knowledge is obviously one source of prevention, and the use of celebrities including high profile athletes has already proved effective in raising the public's awareness of social issues (Brown, Basil, & Bocarnea, 2003). While the baseball player Mark McGuire was breaking homerun records in the late nineties, and was probably best known for his use of steroids, he also acted as a spokesperson against child abuse. As role models, actors and sports figures can be used in mass media campaigns as a means of "involving" (Brown, Basil, & Bocarnea, p. 45) their audiences. As discussed in the chapter about the commercial side of sport, these celebrity role models 'engage' their audiences through forms of identification and a strong sense of intimacy (Brown Basil and Bocarnea refer to this phenomenon as a *parasocial relationship* or *parasocial interaction* with media figures or an "imaginary friendship" [p. 47] that goes beyond straightforward modeling). Brown Basil and Bocarnea cited research that has uncovered, for better or worse, how these idols have induced strong emotional, behavioral and cognitive effects on their recipients. The strong feelings of friendship that youth have with these role models can go beyond simple imitation to an intense sharing of values and beliefs. That is why advertising is so effective. With regard to child abuse, the same principles that the media uses to sell products can and should be used in public service. The more visible the celebrity is, the more powerful the message. For example, as Brown Basil and Bocarnea discovered, Mark McGuire's homerun quest set him up as a suitable spokesperson despite his association with performance enhancing drugs. While the purpose of their research was to investigate the differences between parasocial interaction and observational learning, the underlying message of their research with respect to abuse in youth sport was that using well-known personalities as spokespersons can have far-reaching educational implications. Other, more recent examples of using positive role models in youth sport has been the use of high profile ambassadors such as Joey Cheek, Silken Laumann, Clara Hughes, Dikembe Mutombo, Anni Firesinger and Ian Thorpe in an international effort to support positive values in sport as a means of promoting peace and health. The program is called Right to Play (http://www.righttoplay.com).

CONCLUSION

Donnelly (1997) made a parallel between youth sport, particularly at the elite level, and child labour outside of the world of sport. Attempting to reach the pinnacle of success in one's sport is hard work and long hours, sometimes at a very young age, and under the supervision of others whose careers may be defined by the successes or failures of their protégés. Donnelly perceived adults as frequently exploiting youth for their own personal aggrandizement. Is 'sport-labour' the way individuals involved in youth sport wish to regard youth sport participation? Highly doubtful! More extensive research in the field, both qualitative and quantitative, is needed to clarify the elements at play in this microcosm of experiences. Moreover, further investigation is needed on the victims of abuse--their personalities, motivations, symptoms and coping mechanisms (for example). Research on the victims of abuse in youth sport has been sparse, and is essential if individuals working in youth sport truly value the rights of this population. Children's rights must be respected, or, as Donnelly has implied, participants in youth sports may end up in courtrooms rather than on the playing fields.

REFERENCES

Donnelly, P. (1997). Child labour, sport labour. *International Review for the Sociology of Sport, 32*(4), 389-406.

Fasting, K., Brackenridge, C. H., & Sundgot-Borgen. (2004). Prevalence of sexual harassment among Norwegian female elite athletes in relation to sport type. *International Review for the Sociology of Sport, 39*(4), 373-386.

Fried, G. B. (1996). Strategies for reducing sexual assaults in youth sports. *Journal of Legal Aspects of Sport, 6*(3), 155-168.

Gervis, M., & Dunn, N. (2004). The emotional abuse of elite child athletes by their coaches.

schools and recreational facilities: Implications for developing effective prevention strategies. *Children and Youth Services, 21*(8), 621-642.

Zaichkowsky, L. D. (2000). The Dark Side of Youth Sports: Coaches Sexually Abusing Children. *USA Today Magazine, 128*(2656), 56.

Chapter 4

SPORT PSYCHOLOGY FOR YOUNG ATHLETES

Evidence demonstrates the pressures that young children incur as they begin the pursuit toward excellence in sport (Gould, Damarjian, & Medbery, 1999). These pressures can be internally based for the perfectionist child who dependent on feedback, and striving to meet the expectations of others, may succumb to stress, burnout and overtraining before adolescence. Or, the pressures may emanate from external sources such as parents, peers and coaches whose expectations may be unrealistic and therefore unattainable leading to symptoms of performance anxiety. Gould, Damarjian, and Medbery addressed issues surrounding physically and psychologically driven young athletes who conceivably could have taken control over their lives, or at the very least, could have foreseen the pitfalls of such internal and external pressures had they developed the appropriate skills to handle and respond to such circumstances. These very skills are the core of mental or psychological skill training (PST) in sport psychology.

With reference to sport psychology and youth a number of questions come to mind, (1) Can participation in sport enhance life skills for those youth who take part? (2) Can coaches teach sport psychology skills to young athletes? (3) Can the psychological skills be taught to all children within an education-based curriculum under the rubric of life skill development? (4) Is there any evidence that the latter questions have already been put to test?

The following competencies emerge when addressing the issue of psychological skill training in general and the skills that are used to enhance performance in sport: goal setting, motivation, stress management and arousal regulation, imagery training, cognitive restructuring, and confidence building. Naturally, these strategies are not limited to the purview of sport psychology and elite athletes, but are competencies that I believe should be incorporated into all areas of learning related to preparing children for life. One such area is youth sport. As Smoll and Smith stated, "there is, however, another sport domain that is equally worthy of attention (*besides enhancing performance of elite athletes*), namely, youth sports" (Conroy and Coatsworth as cited by Smoll & Smith, 2001, p. 378).

It generally has been thought that participation in sport in and of itself provides youth with opportunities for self development as they learn team work, how to deal with adversity and success, how to control their emotions, and when to take risks. This notion appears to be a controversial one. From a positive perspective, a study on adolescence and school sports demonstrated that sport involvement can lead to better nutrition, exercise, healthier self-image and reductions in emotional stress and substance abuse (Harrison & Narayan, 2003). This position makes sense if one examines the larger literature on the psychological benefits of physical activity. However, it also has been shown that simply participating in sport does not lead automatically to the development of psychological skills, positive attitudes toward participation, and positive attributions for success (Ronald E. Smith & Smoll, 1997; Smoll & Smith, 2001). A determining factor is how organized youth sport programs are structured by significant adults (e.g., the coach or parent), and how the latter views the teaching of psychological skills. Unfortunately, a supporter of mental skill training in physical education, Sherman (1999) suggested that our society has generally taken a "wait until it breaks" (p. 25) rather than proactive approach to providing children with the necessary psychological tools to navigate through life.

Besides teaching the necessary curriculum subjects in school, the teaching of psychological skills has not been viewed by teachers and teacher training programs as their responsibility, but rather the responsibility of counselors and psychologists (and more often than not, only when a child's problem has been targeted as pathological). And yet, countless children suffer from low self-esteem and confidence, and present to the medical world with various disorders that are stress-based. Psychological skills have become survival skills for all, and are competencies that should be instilled in youth at all levels of education including early childhood. There would be nothing better than preparing children for life's hurdles by providing them with the appropriate strategies and tools inherent to the teachings of sport psychology. After all, only about 98% of children become elite athletes (Gould, Damarjian, & Medbery, 1999). Only recently have those involved with the education of youth, including parents, teachers, and coaches attributed as much value to mental skill training as to the acquisition of other subject matter. Nonetheless, modifying attitudes requires a change in mindset by all stakeholders including the children themselves. As noted by Blom, Hardy, and Joyner (2003), some athletes hold very negative perceptions of sport psychology and toward those who have used sport psychology services. Their work with high school athletes uncovered mixed feelings about and gender differences in attitudes toward sport psychology. However, they did conclude that the adolescents in their study generally supported its use in sport and life. My position is that instilling the competencies as part of the learning process of younger elementary children would make the learning of these skills a natural and accepted process of day-to-day instruction. Early intervention also would help to diminish the stigma of those using sport psychology resources as 'having problems' and sport psychologists' as 'shrinks' -- attitudes that are uninformed and disparaging perceptions of this field.

Generally, coaches have not taken advantage of opportunities to incorporate PST into their instruction at all levels of sport. This is mostly due to lack of training in the psychological aspects of sport (Ronald E. Smith & Smoll, 1997; Smoll & Smith, 2001). Danish and Nellen (1997) pointed out that many high level athletes value the benefits of performance enhancement techniques in other domains of their lives, and have suggested an expansion of the field of sport psychology into other areas of life skill development. The issue is not *whether* these skills can be applied across the lifespan and in venues besides those related to sport and clinical settings, but rather, *how* we educate others to recognize the value of these life enhancement competencies in human development. We already know that participation in sport and exercise has its positive benefits. Adding a new dimension to this experience by introducing PST through a life skills education approach would only enhance these gains. Evidence-based research involving youth is needed in order to evaluate the potential benefits, if any, of early learning and use of these competencies.

SPORT PSYCHOLOGY APPLIED TO YOUTH SPORT

There has been increased interest in research related to psychological skill development in youth sport (Weiss & Raedeke, 2004). In their content analysis of youth sport research from 1982 to 1998, they cited research noting that there were 34 empirical reviews related to this topic—an exponential growth from the previous decade. Hinkle (1994) alleged that the involvement of sport psychologists and sport counselors in school sports programs would enhance children's sport experiences and bring about changing values and attitudes about healthy, active living in youth in addition to other lifestyle changes. In fact, the World Health Organization (1999) has endorsed the teaching of these life skills as a form of enriching human development. Hinkle's thinking was that changes at the intellectual, emotional, and physical level would both carry over into adulthood, and satisfy some of the concerns about growing inactivity and obesity in our youth. Studies on adult populations clearly have demonstrated the benefits of physical activity on cognitive, physical and emotional attributes of the individuals studied (e.g., the benefits of physical activity on depression). Instruction should begin early in a child's life! The questions that need answers to are: *how* and *by whom*? Is it more cost effective or efficient to leave the teaching of such skills to trained psychologists and counselors or to involve classroom teachers in the instruction of these valuable competencies? The issue of crossing professional boundaries is inevitably a sensitive topic.

Lobbying for training in the area of sport psychology for student teachers in physical education as well as providing workshops for coaches should be a primary objective of sport psychology associations worldwide. Education about sport psychology is already in evidence in some countries. For example, the National Coaching Institute of the Coaching Association of Canada (http://www.coach.ca10.5 as part of its requirements for certification, two courses that cover sport psychology—Mental Preparation for Coaches ad Mental Preparation for Athletes. As well, a limited number of teacher education programs in Canada require sport psychology as part of the curriculum in their Bachelor of Arts programs in physical education (e.g., McGill University, University of Toronto, and University of Ottawa). The challenge is to include this knowledge in all programs, and to instill in potential users a deeper understanding of sport psychology theory, principles, and practice so they value its use with youth. In fact, all teachers should try to incorporate elements of PST into their classes or instructional programs even on a limited basis. As Pain and Harwood (2004) suggested, "As players become more familiar with sport psychology at the youth level, they should begin to accept it as a natural part of their development process" (pp. 824-825).

RESEARCH WITH COACHES AS PROVIDERS OF PST

Despite a growing body of research on the benefits of physical activity for children, including the psychological, there has been little evidence-based research related to sport psychology interventions designed for youth. Part of the problem has been that coaches' lack of knowledge about sport psychology makes it difficult not only for them to implement PST within their normal training sessions, but also for sport psychologists to gain entry into the coaches' domain. Pain and Harwood (2004) addressed this very question in their study of the knowledge base and misconceptions of sport psychology held by English soccer coaches and directors (e.g., the sport psychologist as 'shrink'), and their evaluation of the Psychology for Football intervention for coaches, players and staff at the youth sport level of the Football Association of England. Essentially, surveys and interviews revealed that both national and academy coaches as well as youth academy directors and assistant directors (all male, total N = 56) were quite uninformed about such concepts as goal setting, relaxation training, self-talk and use of imagery. Pain and Harwood also felt that lack of awareness about sport psychology obstructed entry by sport psychologists into these youth soccer programs and ultimately, acceptance of sport psychology principles by athletes and their coaches at more elite levels of participation. In fact, results of interviews uncovered six particular areas of concern regarding coaches' understandings and perceptions of sport psychology: negative perceptions, lack of knowledge, use for both players and coaches, lack of clarity of the role of and services provided by sport psychologists, practical limitations, and the perceived worth of sport psychology. Financial constraints and misconceptions of what the field had to offer also surfaced as major barriers. In Pain and Harwood's investigation, goal setting and team building followed by motivation and concentration training were the best-understood concepts while biofeedback and hypnosis the least understood. Emotional control, self-talk, relaxation training, and confidence building also were toward the lower end of the scale of coaches' knowledge. The data of this study underscored the fact that the field of sport psychology is in need of a major promotional boost if it is to reach the youth sport level of participation where its benefits are more far-reaching than simply enhancing sport performance (i.e., many of these skills are life skills). That sport psychology was viewed as 'common sense' was a repeatedly emerging theme in the study (50% of respondents) as were other negative perceptions of sport psychology ("the word psychology was taboo", Pain & Harwood, p. 819). Clearly, coaches need some training in the theory, principles and applications of sport psychology.

Harwood, Middlemas, and Reeves (2005) reported on the results of a mental skills training intervention for young soccer players (ages under 9–12). In carrying out the intervention, the researchers referred to coaches' establishing a mental skills climate that promoted psycho-social development in addition to the teaching of physical skills. Related research had indicated that coaches were not well prepared to teach mental skills, and that programs should be designed to assist coaches in acquiring the knowledge and skills to implement such programs. The premise of their work was similar to that of Smoll and Smith's (e.g., see Smoll & Smith, 2001 for a detailed description of the CET procedures and underlying theory)— train the coaches in sport psychology to enable them to create an instructional climate that reinforces psychological competencies in children. Harwood, Middlemas, and Reeves' goal was not only to teach coaches concepts related to mental skills training and to enhance coaching efficacy in terms of developing these mental skills in athletes, but also to evaluate whether the athletes were seen as improving their mental skill responses in the training sessions.

Characteristically, three of the four coaches had very little knowledge of sport psychology besides introductory courses. Three, 60-90 minutes sessions took place every 2 weeks. In the training sessions, coaches focused on what Harwood, Middlemas, and Reeves (2005) called the "5 C's" —Commitment (e.g., encouraging persistence, engagement and approach behaviour), Communication (e.g., asking questions, accepting feedback, encouraging team mates), Concentration (e.g., maintaining focus on task, eye contact),

*C*ontrol (e.g., quick recovery from errors, managing emotions), and *C*onfidence (e.g., does not fear making mistakes, exuding 'presence'). Coaches were introduced to behaviors and strategies that would help foster the development of each of these 'C's' in players. First, coaches were familiarized with concepts of commitment and motivation. They were asked to integrate 'commitment' coaching behaviors over the next five coaching sessions. Instruction in and practice of each 'C' continued until all "5 C's" had been integrated over four months.

Coaches evaluated themselves on a session by session basis on how well they felt they implemented the "5 C's" strategies over five practice sessions, and how much players showed "5 C" responses in their session. Their coaching efficacy was tracked every two weeks. Results showed how commitment and communication behaviors both elevated confidence and players' training responses in other areas. Coaches reported using less concentration and control behaviors. Generally, the researchers uncovered positive use of the "5 C's" by athletes. They did question whether the intervention would have long-term effects, and called for coaches to become more amenable to helping athletes develop and practice self-control skills in practice rather than inappropriately leaving it only for competition. Being a developmentally based study, Harwood, Middlemas, and Reeves (2005) emphasized that future interventions be designed in a developmentally appropriate manner. Basically, they expressed a need for continued investigation into what are appropriate competencies for particular age groups as well as the refinement of teaching strategies designed to enhance coaches' understandings of sport psychology concepts.

Smith and Smoll (1997) and Smith, Smoll, and Barnett (1995) directly observed how youth coaches handled the psychological component of sport following relevant workshops. They examined coaches' use of positive reinforcement, reaction to errors, and support measures, and evaluated both coaches' and children's recall of the frequency of occurrence of these coaching behaviors. The athletes' feelings of enjoyment, performance anxiety, self-esteem and attitudes concerning coaching practice were also investigated in a series of studies (Smoll & Smith, 2001). The only variable that interacted with winning was coaching behavior while encouragement and positive reinforcement were linked to positive outcomes. Children enjoyed their sports experiences more when coaches used basic psychological principles of motivation. Interestingly, Smith and Smoll reported that the children were more conscious of the coaches' use of the psychological techniques than were the coaches themselves suggesting that interventions should emphasize reflective practice in coaches. The findings of their initial investigation led to the development of Coach Effectiveness Training programs (CET). The emphasis of CET is to create positive coaching and the mastery learning environments with a focus on teamwork, having fun, effort, self-esteem, self-regulation, positive attitudes and sportspersonship (Smith, Smoll & Curtis as cited in Ronald E. Smith & Smoll, 1997; Smoll & Smith, 2001). A major goal of CET is to provide social support for young athletes.

As explained by Smoll and Smith (2001), the theoretical and research paradigm for CET is: "coach's behavior → athletes' perceptions and recall → athletes' evaluative reactions" (p. 379). Further, assessment of CET programs has involved examining changes in coaching behavior and children's attitudes about the coach, peers, and sport experience; increases in self-esteem; decreases in performance anxiety; sport adherence; and reactions to coaches trained in CET. Studies by Smith and Smoll have uncovered the merits of CET. Essentially, CET-trained coaches applied what they learned in the workshops they attended, and the children of these coaches enjoyed their sport experiences more than did those in control groups. Most importantly, as related to PST, results of Smith and Smoll's research efforts have uncovered increases in self-esteem and decreases in performance anxiety (Smith, Smoll, & Barnett; Smith, Smoll, Barnett & Everett as cited in Ronald E. Smith & Smoll, 1997; Smoll & Smith, 2001). Essentially, coaches' developing basic awareness of fundamental principles of motivation made a difference in the psychological development of children consequently demonstrating that using sport psychology with youth does not have to be complicated to achieve benefits. Unfortunately, more often than not, coaches as well as athletes perceive sport psychology principles as beyond their grasp or something that they fear or attach a sense of mystique to. Smith and Smoll encouraged continued research in the area of CET and youth sport using different populations. Their belief has been that because youth sport coaches play such a significant role in the lives of children, the latter have the potential of furthering not only technical skills, but also attitudes, values, and psychological well being. The coach-athlete relationship is critical to this development.

In one particular study in the area, Smith, Smoll, and Barnett (1995) investigated the effects of CET on children's sport performance anxiety. Stress management is a strategic skill related to performance enhancement in both sport and life. Incorporating instruction in how to deal with anxiety and stress is valuable and practical information that children should be taught at a young age. Stress is the root of countless problems--physical, cognitive and emotional, and yet, teaching children how to deal with it generally has been ignored in education, let alone sport. Studies have shown that many children quit sports because of anxiety surrounding fear of failure, unattainable expectations, peer or adult pressure or criticism (Smith, Smoll, & Barnett). If a long-term societal goal is to keep children active, adherence to physical activity pursuits is fundamental. One way of increasing youth participation is by addressing psychological issues such as stress management with the expectation that competencies learned through sport would transfer to other venues in life.

In Smith, Smoll and Barnett's (1995) study, youth baseball coaches attended CET sessions where they were taught both how to lessen anxiety in youngsters and how to model appropriate behavior in response to stress. The premise of the study was that CET would reduce performance anxiety in children and provide them with coping skills. One hundred fifty-two boys (62 experimental, 90 control), ages 10 – 12 years, participated in the research. All the coaches were male with an average of 7 years of coaching experience. The CET program was held two weeks before the season started and lasted roughly 2.5 hours. Coaches were taught not only the psychological skills, but were trained to monitor their own behavior throughout the season as a form of reflective practice. Following the 10-week season, scores for the experimental group on the Sport Anxiety Scale (Smith, Smoll, & Schutz as cited in Smith, Smoll, & Barnett) and the Sport Competition Anxiety Test (Martens as cited in Smith, Smoll, & Barnett) significantly improved over those who had the untrained coaches. In other words, those players whose coaches had attended the CET workshops showed decreases in performance anxiety by the end of the season. Additionally, the children in the experimental group were reported to have understood the positive, cognitive-behavioral cues of the coaches who had attended the CET workshops (e.g., "circle how often your coach encouraged you after you made mistakes", Smith, Smoll, & Barnett, p. 131). The boys also indicated that their coaches were better teachers. Both groups enjoyed their baseball experience. However, surprisingly, there was no correlation between performance anxiety scores and team success. Smith, Smoll and Barnett attributed this finding to the unstable nature of the skill level of young athletes. All in all, the work of Smith and Smoll has demonstrated that coaches can have an effect on the psychological well being of young players. Acknowledging these effects and the results of interventions like CET while also utilizing this knowledge for the betterment of young athletes should be the goal of all youth sport programs. A coach can be an influential persona in the life of a child.

Advancing the CET work of Smith and Smoll, Coatsworth and Conroy (2006) reported on a study in which four female youth sport coaches underwent a social support training program where they were taught skills necessary for providing a supportive and mastery-oriented instructional climate. In the control condition two female coaches and a male coach attended an injury prevention workshop. The primary purpose of the study was to examine whether the psychosocial coaching intervention would lead to increases in the self-esteem of 135 mixed gender (52 boys, 83 girls), swimmers (ages 7 – 18). Observations showed that the behavior of the coaches in the experimental condition positively changed. Unlike Smith and Smoll's (1997) findings, they found the following: long-term results did not lead to significant changes in self-esteem based on coach training over the 7-week period (keep in mind that self-esteem is a fairly stable factor), results indicated that age and initial levels of self esteem moderated the results (i.e., those swimmers who were younger than 11 years old and had initially low levels of self-esteem showed the greatest gains). Gender also surfaced as a mediating factor as only the girls with initial levels of low self-esteem were significantly influenced by the trained coaches. Most importantly, Coatsworth and Conroy's study demonstrated that interventions with coaches were effective in terms of both changing coaching behavior and having positive effects on the younger athletes under their supervision. The ramifications of their findings have implications for young children's continued participation in physical activity. The diverse findings on gender as related to self-esteem between Coatsworth and Conroy's and Smith and Smoll's work merits further investigation. Coach gender as well as how the self-esteem measures were utilized may have been factors in the respective analyses.

Using the previous study as a springboard to further work in the area, Conroy and Coatsworth also examined the effects of CET training on fear of failure (Performance Failure Appraisal Inventory, Conroy & Coatsworth, 2004). While coaching behavior changed, analyses did not reveal a significant effect on fear of failure over the 7-week period for either boys or girls. The stability and complex structure of fear of failure and the many factors that may influence it outside of the coach-athlete relationship (e.g., type of sport, sample diversity, length of treatment) conceivably were responsible for the lack of positive findings.

Unfortunately, the number of studies demonstrating the mediating effects of coaching behavior on youth is quite limited. For this reason, Conroy and Coatsworth (2006) concluded with prudent advice to practitioners that is worth sharing. They recommended that "youth sport organizations and school boards consider incorporating such programs for new and experienced youth sport coaches alike while researchers work to establish the necessary conditions for efficacious training programs that enhance youth development" (p. 212). The basic premise of Conroy and Coatsworth's (2004) study and Smith and Smoll's work has been that that an "important instructor" (Conroy and Coatsworth, p. 195, in this case the coach) can affect change. Perhaps interventions with youth, and not only their coaches, would have more of an impact on outcome measures such as fear of failure and potentially other psychological variables that influence children's success in both sport and life. If implemented, close attention must be paid to the developmental appropriateness of these interventions. There is much valuable research to be done on this issue! A discussion of interventions and research specifically directed at youth follows.

INTERVENTIONS WITH YOUTH

The majority of mental skills training work directly targeted at youth primarily has been carried out with adolescents. Possible reasons include the fact that elementary school programs in some countries do not require physical education, or the position that younger children do not have the cognitive capacity to handle such abstract concepts as imagery use or relaxation training. I heartily challenge the latter attitude. As mentioned frequently throughout the book, the early years of a child's life are the formative ones and the time for children to develop positive life skills. If interventions are developmentally appropriate, they should work.

a. Adolescents

Harwood, Cumming, and Fletcher (2004) looked at the relationship between dispositional goal orientation and the use of such psychological skills as imagery, goal setting, relaxation and positive self-talk (a particularly undeveloped area of research). They hypothesized that those adolescents with a healthy (high) balance of task and ego goal orientations would use significantly more PST strategies in game and practice situations than those athletes with low task and ego goal orientations. Nicholls' (1984) Achievement Goal Theory served as the theoretical foundation for this study. Basically, Achievement Goal Theory addresses the motivations that individuals hold for why they participate   sport. Two distinct motivational orientations are underscored—task-orientation, where individuals focus on the process and personal successes and ego-orientation, characterized by participants whose will is to better one's opponent and 'win at all costs'. Five hundred and seventy three elite athletes (ages 14 - 20) from a broad range of sports participated in Harwood, Cumming and Fletcher's research. Participants included a 3:1 ratio of females to males. The researchers administered the Perceptions of Success Questionnaire used to assess goal orientation (Roberts, Treasure, & Balague as cited in Harwood, Cumming and Fletcher) and the Test of Performance Strategies that evaluates use of psychological skills (TOPS, Thomas et al. as cited in Harwood, Cumming and Fletcher). Those athletes who held high-task/moderate ego-orientations used psychological skills significantly more than athletes who were low-task/high ego- and moderate-task/low ego-oriented. Interestingly, males reported having a significantly higher ego orientation yet used relaxation and self-talk strategies more often than females. All in all, Harwood, Cumming and Fletcher's findings supported the assumption that an appropriate motivational orientation plays a role in whether sports participants adopt PST as part of their training regimen. In addition, a high task-orientation, more characteristic of mastery learning environments, appeared to be an important element in most cases of PST with the exception of relaxation strategies.

In an earlier study, Harwood and his research colleagues (as cited in Harwood, Cumming, & Fletcher, 2004) discovered that Canadian, provincial level swimmers with moderate task/high-ego orientation used imagery strategies more frequently than other combinations of task- and ego-orientations. A second study in Britain confirmed these results. The researchers concluded that the ego-oriented athlete used imagery primarily to enhance athletic skill, while the more task-oriented athletes practiced imagery for personal mastery (i.e., confidence building, positive self talk). If adopting such psychological skills enhances sport performance, and more importantly transfers to important life skills, there is cause for including both a mastery learning environment and a mental training component in youth sport programs regardless of level of participation. Child development theory would support early PST interventions. Yet, much needed research is needed to confirm this claim. Harwood, Cumming, and Fletcher also provided some useful practical information on how to establish sport environments that maximize the balance of personal goal types.

In a related study, Miller and Donohue (2003) evaluated the benefits of PST with 90 long distance runners evenly distributed by gender, and ranging in age from 14-18. Their goal was to examine whether mental training would enhance actual performance. Participants listened to a 3-minute recording after preliminary baseline trials and prior to a second experimental run. Experimental conditions included: listening to motivational and running techniques, listening to music, and no sound. Personalized recordings were designed around individual runner's evaluations of a list of motivational and instructional statements. The latter also selected their music. Following the second run, athletes evaluated their satisfaction with the respective interventions.

Findings indicated that those in Conditions 1 and 2 significantly improved their run performance over those who listened to nothing. Listening to the motivational and running technique recordings resulted in the highest mean improvement times. Most importantly, the runners' feelings of perceived improvement and satisfaction with the interventions were positive. Essentially, the mental training strategies used in this study proved valuable for this young, non-elite set of athletes. No gender effects emerged. Further research on the effectiveness of mental training techniques with younger samples using varying methods of introducing the techniques and across different sports would be useful information for those strictly interested in the relationship between mental training and performance. It is quite remarkable that Miller and Donohue (2003) demonstrated that merely a 3-minute recording could make a significant difference in performance. They did not compare the motivational and technique recordings as the latter were always presented in combination. Generalization of the intervention's benefits to other behavior was not an objective of Miller and Donohue's work, but may be worthy of study by those with an interest in life skill development.

Another area of mental skills training, guided goal setting based on social cognitive theory, has proven to be successful in changing adolescents' eating and physical activity habits (EatFit intervention, Shilts, Horowitz, & Townsend, 2004). It was Shilts, Horowitz, and Townsend's belief that goal setting, with its requirements for abstract reasoning, could be taught to adolescents if the latter were guided through the process and asked to select goals prepared by adults. Their project evolved into a impressive website with both student and teacher materials (see www.eatfit.net). As a aside, although there is not much evidence to support my belief, I would think that more simplified goal setting strategies also could be used successfully with younger children if taught in a developmentally appropriate manner and similarly guided through the process. The EatFit web program (www.eatfit.net/program/program.html) involved a 9-weeks intervention requiring students to interact with materials on the project website. A diary, available on the website, monitored eating and physical activity habits. The computer program was designed to provide participants with feedback and goal options from which they chose one (e.g., "Eat a breakfast cereal with less than 10g of sugar per serving, 3 mornings a week", Shilts, Horowitz, & Townsend, p. 155). Participants printed out, and signed a personal contract for behavior change. Rewards were built into the program as were social support and other forms of motivation. Preliminary evaluations of the guided goal setting intervention with low SES, ethnically mixed, Grade 8 children demonstrated the success of this interactive and innovative program both in terms of altering behavior and providing the participants with awareness of goal setting. As Shilts, Horowitz, and Townsend suggested, more research is necessary to evaluate whether similar benefits can be achieved with older and younger youth. This innovative and interactive approach to instruction in goal setting with youth has limitless applications. In light of considerable concern about obesity and youth, this program is a valuable one for teachers and possibly parents. Take a look at the website!

In other goal setting work with adolescents, Danish and Nellen (1997) taught 'at-risk' youth psychological skills through their ongoing sports participation. Their goal was two-fold: 1) to enhance the youngsters' lives by helping them achieve higher levels of proficiency which the researchers hoped would be transferable to real life situations, and 2) to increase the participants' chances of breaking through social barriers imposed by negative influences in their inner city surroundings through means other than becoming a highly gifted professional athlete. Clearly, learning to use PST strategies in different situations that have been taught through sport could have a far-reaching influence across a broad base of youth. Danish and Nellen so aptly pointed out that, "what has been overlooked by these critics (of the value of sport) is how sport *can* provide a setting where *life skills* are learned" (p. 101). They reported on the benefits of "life skills, sports-based programs" (p. 101) that they designed and implemented for a sample of at-risk youth (see http://www.lifeskills.vcu.edu/index.html). The objective of these skill-building and mental training programs was to use the popularity of sport already evident in this community of disadvantaged youth to instill in them competencies that they ultimately could use beyond sport. Learning personal development competencies was as important as learning how to play and compete. Danish and Nellen stressed that the sport experience, not sport itself, unearths important life skills. This was the rationale behind Danish and his colleagues' developing the GOAL program, a highly-funded intervention designed to teach adolescents skills of goal setting, self-regulation and confidence building (Danish & Nellen).

Peer tutoring was used in the GOAL program as older, specially trained and high ability high school students taught younger high school or middle school students during the 10-hours, 10-sessions intervention. The program can be taught in schools or other venues (the "Going for the Goal" activity guides are available through the center's website). Use of high school students as tutors was deliberate in that coming from similar backgrounds as the participants, they served as good role models. There has been a great deal of evidence in the peer tutoring literature that peer tutors also enhance their own knowledge and competencies as well as their teaching skills (Baron, 1991). Essentially, the program was designed to teach adolescents positive goal setting skills related to their future careers, hobbies, friends and families ("dare to dream," p. 104). They were challenged to specify reachable goals and the steps toward attaining them—a task that from my own experience adults find tough, but insightful. Finally, they were asked to identify barriers to reaching their goals, and not only how to overcome these barriers through problem solving strategies, but also how to reach out to others for support in attaining their goals (participant's supportive "dream team", p. 104). Adolescents were compelled to think about how issues such as drug use, delinquency, personal control and self-confidence, and school dropout may impede their achieving their goals. In the final session, they played a game that required applying what they learned.

Evaluations of the workshops were positive (Danish & Nellen, 1997). Feedback from participants indicated that they learned the information and how to set and achieve goals. School attendance was higher than that of a control group, and males who participated in GOAL reported less substance abuse and lower incidents of violence and other negative behaviors. Those who partook in the life skills program thought it was "fun, useful, important and something that would be helpful for their friends" (Meyer, Burgess, & Danish as cited in Danish & Nellen, p. 106).

The blending of sports and life skills led the Life Skills Center staff to develop the SUPER program that was modeled on the GOAL program. Youth were taught to become more task- rather than ego-oriented and to be less concerned about social comparison. Bettering oneself in sport and life rather than outdoing one's opponent has been the motto of SUPER. Subsequent development of the program included adding imagery training as well as anger management components. Danish (Danish, 1996) reported changes in confidence and dependency needs by way of the SUPER program. The most important lesson learned was the ability to transfer skills to everyday life. Transferring knowledge and skills to different arenas of life, in addition to learning to accept one's mistakes, may be a slow process. However, with support and guidance from the leaders, participants were afforded supervised opportunities to practice these life skills.

The non-sport specific GOAL program has been implemented successfully by others (O'Hearn & Gatz as cited in Papacharisis, Goudas, Danish, & Theodorakis, 2005). However, there has been little reported on the effects of the SUPER program. Papacharisis, Goudas, Danish, and Theodorakis carried out one such study by examining the participants' (ages 10-12) knowledge of life skills, transferability of these skills, self-assessments regarding the latter, and sport performance. The hypotheses supported the use of a brief SUPER intervention held during practice sessions (8,15-minute sessions). The SUPER studies were conducted in Greece, and involved athletes who had already competed at a competitive level for at least two years. One study included 40 female volleyball players while the other involved 32 male soccer players. Participants were randomly assigned, and fairly evenly distributed into experimental (skill training and SUPER program) and control (skill training only) groups. Pre- and post-tests included *Knowledge* of goal setting and one's belief in their ability to set goals, problem solve and think positively. In both studies, a Group X Time interaction demonstrated a significant difference between the experimental and control groups on *Knowledge* and self-beliefs with the experimental group outperforming the control group. The experimental group also did significantly better on all of the volleyball skills. For the soccer intervention, post-test performance scores for the experimental group also were significantly higher than for the control group. Papacharisis, Goudas, Danish, and Theodorakis' work demonstrated that incorporating a PST program into a program designed to teach sport skills enhances both knowledge of life skills and targeted sport skills—a noteworthy finding. It would have been particularly informative to examine whether these life skills transferred to contexts other than the targeted sports.

Finally, as related to psychological skills training, GetPsychedSports.org has as its mission to "bring positive change to organized sport from grade school through high school by:

- "Building self-worth for good mental health
- Calming the atmosphere around organized sport

- Enhancing personal performance in all areas of life" (GetPsychedSports.org)

I have been impressed with the applied work this group has carried out in the area of mental training for high school athletes. The organization's website contains an abundance of valuable curriculum materials and resources for educators, coaches, parents and athletes. The philosophy of GetPsychedSports.org, like mine, is that mental training competencies are life skills that should be taught early.

b. Young Children

I have worked in the area of child development, and have focused most of my research efforts over my career on elementary children. On reviewing the literature for this chapter, I found it somewhat disheartening that the bulk of work on mental training and school-age children had been carried out with high school and college students. Short of that, work in the performance enhancement area naturally had centered on elite or competitive athletes. There are, however, some researchers in the field who have directed their attention to younger children (e.g., Maureen Weiss at the University of Virginia, Chris Harwood of Loughheed University in the U.K., Terry Orlick of the University of Ottawa, and Dan Gould of Michigan State University).

Owing to the limited amount of research related to PST and young sport participants, for this chapter, I have turned to more general research related to teaching psychological skills to young children. Successful attempts to instill these competencies in children in diverse settings and subject areas augurs well for training youngsters to transfer these tools to everyday life. After all, the mantra of this chapter has been that teaching children psychological skills is not exclusively for enhancing performance in sport, but rather for inculcating in children life skills that will serve them over a lifespan.

Relaxation training is one such skill. It has been used regularly in sport psychology particularly in concert with other competencies like imagery. In fact, research has shown that relaxation exercises performed prior to practicing other psychological skills enhances the effects of the latter. Armstrong, Collins, Greene, and Panzironi (1988) looked at different modes of relaxation training on children's motor functioning the belief being that different types of stress management would have a differential impact. For example, progressive relaxation techniques have been linked with reduction in muscle tension while more cognitively based techniques like meditation and distraction control have been thought to 'quiet' the mind. Armstrong, Collins, Greene, and Panzironi cited work in other fields where relaxation training had been implemented successfully to lower arousal and tension in children in a variety of situations (e.g., dental visits, undergoing cancer treatments or surgery). As a life skill, relaxation training has already proven to be effective as an arousal and anxiety reducing competency. Using this evidence, Armstrong, Collins, Greene, and Panzironi compared the effects of visual imagery, progressive relaxation or verbal instructions on somatic, motor and cognitive arousal incurred by test anxious children. It was hypothesized that progressive relaxation would work best with somatic arousal (i.e., physical) while visual imagery would be more efficacious with the more cognitively based forms of arousal (e.g., worry). Thirty, Grade 4 – 6 children (12 boys, 18 girls) participated in the study. A requirement was that they had to have been diagnosed as test anxious. The children were assigned to one of three conditions—progressive muscle relaxation, guided visual imagery, and attention control (verbal prompts to 'relax'). Physiological and self-report measures as well as scores on Spielberger's State-Trait Anxiety Inventory for Children (Speilberger, Edwards, Montuori, & Lushene, 1970) served as indicators of the success of the respective treatments. Participants underwent a 10 − 12 minutes treatment phase in which they were trained in one of the three relaxation techniques. Data on additional performance measures was collected including skills that required fine motor control and mathematical problem solving. Significant differences surfaced for all treatments from pre- to post-treatment. However, there were no differences reported across the treatments. Likely explanations included the short duration of the treatments and ceiling effects. The interventions did not influence mathematical performance, but significantly affected motor performance from pre- to post-intervention. Again, there were no significant main effects triggered by the respective interventions. The researchers' hypothesis about the *"specific effects"* (p. 314) of varying relaxation training modalities was not supported with the exception of the attention control group (i.e., those prompted to relax). The latter showed significant decreases in motor performance over the other interventions. The findings on motor control merit further investigation with a longer treatment phase. Understandably, it would appear from the results of this study that one has to facilitate young children's understanding that the relaxation training skills can be transferred to other situations.

Examining stress management procedures with young children in a school setting, Norlander, Moås, and Archer (2005) uncovered positive effects. They evaluated whether primary and secondary school children could use relaxation procedures to block out in-class noise and to strengthen their powers of concentration. Despite the relatively short, 4-week intervention, both reductions in the level of classroom noise and increases in the capacity to concentrate were reported demonstrating the influential effects of relaxation training in both distraction control and behavior.

If one of our objectives as educators, coaches, or parents is to develop in children a sense of control over their choices and life direction, then teaching them how to set goals at an early age should be a priority. Palmer and Wehmeyer (2003) expressed the belief that, "... starting the process of becoming self-determined before adolescence gives added time for building the children's capacity for choice, decision making, goal setting and problem solving that are essential for later self-determination" (p. 116). Interestingly, what Palmer and Wehmeyer suggested traverses the realms of motivation and related goal setting and self-regulation, as well as cognitive skills like problem solving that are essential life skills that should be taught in the early years. They suggested taking a developmental approach to the teaching of mental skills to young children. Palmer and Wehmeyer utilized Self-Determination Theory (Deci & Ryan, 1985) as the foundation of their work. Their model of teaching was based on the Self-Determination Model of Instruction (Mithaug, Wehmeyer, Agran, Martin, & Palmer, 1998; Wehmeyer, Palmer, Agran, Mithaug, & Martin, 2000 as cited in Palmer & Wehmeyer), which appears to mirror the more constructivist approaches to teaching that allow students to self-direct the learning process to a some extent (e.g., Vygotsky, Piaget).

Very young children can be guided in the process of goal setting as demonstrated by previous work with children as young as age 5 (e.g., Guevremont, Osne, & Stokes and Nicholls & Miller as cited by Palmer & Wehmeyer, 2003). The earlier work cited by Palmer and Wehmeyer served as a springboard for their testing the *Self-Determined Learning Model of Instruction* with 50 children from K-3 (mean age = 7.92 years). Most of the participants were special needs children. In the Self-Determined Learning Model of Instruction, students were instructed to set goals by asking themselves such questions as, "What do I want to learn? What do I know about it now? What must change for me to learn what I don't know? What can I do to make this happen?" (Palmer & Wehmeyer, 2003, p. 116). In answering these questions, and through teacher guidance, children were taught to set goals and to follow up on the goal setting by making decisions for themselves. In Phase 2, students generated a plan. Again, responding to questions such as, "What can I do to learn what I don't know? What could keep me from taking action? What can I do to remove these barriers? When will I take action" (p. 117) directed the learning process. Using the Self-determined Learning Model of Instruction and in order to meet Palmer and Wehmeyer's objectives, students were required to problem solve, set goals, plan their course of action, and re-evaluate the process (Phase 3—"what have I learned", p. 118). Self-regulation was an underlying objective. This is a life skill that can be taught to young children if the sequence, materials and types of questions are designed in a developmentally appropriate manner as Palmer and Wehmeyer did. For example, children answered the questions in empty shapes on a flowchart provided to them. The flowchart made the problem solving process more concrete. Using materials provided by the research team, trained teachers implemented the goal-setting program. Both anecdotal and quantitative assessments (e.g., *Goal Attainment Scaling* or GAS) were used to evaluate the success of the program. Results across all grades and content areas revealed that the students exceeded teachers' expectations. Furthermore, the children showed improvement on three of the four questions asked at pre- and post-test (i.e., knowledge of the words 'goal' and 'interest', and goal examples), and as reported, generally "felt good about meeting their goals, and many students had ideas for other goals to achieve" (Palmer & Wehmeyer, p. 123). Generally, the levels of motivation to learn and achieve increased for these children. Teachers also reported changes in students' general behavior and achievement subsequent to the intervention that further supported its benefits. What a wonderful accomplishment in developing self-regulatory behavior —and, with very young children having disabilities! This work demonstrated that goal setting could be accomplished with young children. The take-home message is that coaches and teachers should not hesitate in implementing basic goal setting strategies in their instructional programs.

Another important psychological skill is the use of imagery. Similar to the previous study on goal setting, imagery training has been taught successfully to elementary children outside of the sports arena and in the classroom (Borduin, Borduin, & Manley, 1994). In the Borduins' work, children were trained in imagery strategies designed to enhance their reading comprehension. Their rationale was that if children 'construct' their own meanings of what they read their comprehension of the material would improve. They demonstrated this by conducting a study with 28, Grade 2 students who were randomly assigned to four groups—Group 1: the imagery training group (IT) who were taught to make images of the text and visual and verbal accounts of the images, Groups 2 and 3: the corrective feedback groups (CF-A and CF-B [two different teachers]), and Group 4: the no instruction group (NI) who read text on their own. The interventions for groups 1, 2, and 3 took place for 30 minutes once a week over a 6 weeks period. Post-test and follow-up assessments included reading a text and answering questions designed to evaluate inference and detail. Results revealed significant effects for training. Both the IT and CF-B group had higher inference scores than the CF-A and NI groups. In time, Borduin, Borduin and Manley reported, the CF-B scores declined to a level equivalent to the NI group. The children who used imagery in their reading also were able to remember more details than the other groups. The researchers concluded that imagery was an effective tool for increasing comprehension of text. Most importantly, Borduin, Borduin and Manley demonstrated that Grade 2 children could become skilled at and apply imagery. This is a practical finding for those interested in introducing the use of imagery as a life- or sport-related skill with young children.

In additional work that supported the use of imagery with younger children (Grades 4 and 6), Lohaus, Klein-Hebling, Vogele, and Kuhn-Hennighausen (2001) revealed that imagery-based relaxation was effective in reducing physiological measures of arousal and in enhancing mood and physical well-being over 5, 30 minute training sessions. Imagery-based relaxation was compared to progressive relaxation and a neutral story. Based on previous research that uncovered the benefits of using imagery on physiological measures, Lohaus, Klein-Hebling, Vogele, and Kuhn-Hennighausen included an imagery-based relaxation component. Imagery involved having the participants visualize himself or herself as a butterfly flying to various "peaceful places" (p. 200). Self-ratings were taken before and after pre-treatment baseline, following the intervention and during the post-treatment baseline phase. Physiological data was gathered during each phase. Both relaxation training procedures and the neutral story were conveyed by audiotape. Results uncovered similar patterns for the imagery-based relaxation training and neutral condition while progressive muscle relaxation actually led to increases in heart rate (as suggested by the researchers, possibly through activation of muscles in progressive relaxation where muscles are tensed, then released). There were no differences in mood ratings across treatments following training albeit mood was enhanced. Similar to work I carried out with children using the slow-moving martial art of Tai Chi (see Baron, 1998; Baron & Faubert, 2005), it may have been possible, as suggested by the researchers, that ceiling effects had been reached on the self-ratings before the treatments began therefore diminishing the treatment effects. Lohaus, Klein-Hebling, Vogele, and Kuhn-Hennighausen also pointed out that the number of treatment sessions was quite minimal limiting effects either by condition or time. Their findings lead to replicating the study with children in Grades 4 and 6 in which treatments were compared over five and 10 sessions (Lohaus & Klein-Hessling, 2003). The number of exercises per session also was increased. An additional treatment, solving arithmetic problems, was added with the expectation that this intervention would in fact bring on tension. This study had similar elements to that of Armstrong, Collins, Greene, & Panzironi (1988) alluded to earlier. Physiological and self-report data was collected. Again, measures indicated no differences across progressive relaxation, imagery-based relaxation and reading, nor did length of treatment make a difference. Similar to the previous study, there were no gender or grade effects. Solving the arithmetic problems caused some tension and decreases in positive mood. Although results did not support extending the number of treatments or long-term effects, a good follow-up study might be to examine the possible transfer of relaxation skills taught on a *daily* basis to stressful situations similar to the problem-solving situation in the Lohaus and Klein-Hessling work. Despite results indicating the benefits of a relaxation and/or mood enhancement as a form of 'time-out' for children regardless of treatment, of some significance regarding the use of imagery-based relaxation with elementary age children was Lohaus et al.'s conclusion that "... children may benefit from relaxation training and that relaxation instructions may induce calmness even in young children" (p. 205).

Finally, there have been successful attempts at using imagery training with young children having motor disorders (Wilson, Thomas, & Maruff, 2002). Wilson, Thomas and Maruff compared the utility of imagery training, perceptual motor training and a control treatment in developing motor skills in 54 children, ages 7-12, diagnosed with developmental coordination disorder and mild motor clumsiness. The rationale for their study was that motor disabilities have the potential of impairing academic achievement and quality of life. Wilson, Thomas and Maruff reviewed the reported successes of using imagery training in the rehabilitation of adult and child athletes with motor injuries, and hypothesized that there would be similar improvements using motor imagery training with children having motor disorders. Imagery training in this study involved the children's interacting with a computer-driven imagery program developed by the researchers. The program involved imagery exercises (external and internal visualization), modelling and a relaxation component over 5 weeks of one-hour sessions. Participants in this treatment condition were compared on a standardized measure of motor function to those in a traditional perceptual-motor group (hopping, skipping, jumping and marching activities) and a no treatment control group. The researchers stated that the positive results on imagery training alone were "remarkable" (p. 495) and "intriguing" (p. 497) particularly considering the shortness of the intervention. Participants in this condition significantly improved their movement assessment scores from pre- to post-test comparing favorably with traditional methods. The results demonstrated the strength of mentally rehearsing motor movements with the most severe cases, and also underscored the utility of a computer-driven intervention that could be implemented anywhere. These findings highlighted the important link between mind and body. Additionally, the findings of Wilson, Thomas and Maruff's work provided further evidence not only that imagery training works, but also that it is effective with young children.

Despite various positive findings, the question still remains open for further study as to whether imagery training can be used to enhance children's performance in a variety of life activities as well as in sport. Lohaus et al. (2001) and Lohaus and Klein-Hessling (2003) expressed some hesitation surrounding young children's motivation to use more static relaxation strategies despite the fact that research has demonstrated its effectiveness with kindergarten children if the appropriate conditions are present for this age group. It was precisely this thinking that served as a catalyst for my choosing Tai Chi in my studies on anxiety reduction and mood enhancement. It is a form of relaxation through movement. Tai Chi practice was very well-received by upper elementary children (Baron, 1998) and proved beneficial for hyperactivity and heightened anxiety (Baron & Faubert, 2005).

More broad-based mental training programs also have been implemented with children. For example, Mamassis and Doganis (2004) carried out the Mental Training Program (MTP) the goals of which were to enhance the performance of four tennis players (mean ages 13.2 and 15.2). This is one of the few studies targeted specifically at performance enhancement of elite young athletes. Mamassis and Doganis' season-long intervention (25 weeks) embraced most of the elements of a mental training program—goal setting, positive self-talk and cognitive restructuring, attention and concentration, arousal regulation and imagery training. In comparison to a control group, results demonstrated the effectiveness of the treatment particularly as related to anxiety control and increased self-confidence. The researchers proposed that coaches and trainers include elements of PST in their training sessions. In particular, they highlighted the use of stress management techniques and goal setting, and emphasized the need for coaches to focus on self-efficacy beliefs and confidence particularly before competitions. In an earlier work, Atienza, Balaguer, and Garcia-Merita (1998) demonstrated the effectiveness of modeling and imagery training with 12 female tennis players as young as nine while Li-Wei, Qi-Wei, Orlick, and Zitzelsberger (1992) reported positive results of using imagery with table tennis players ages 7 to 10.

Readers are referred to Sherman's description of an integrated physical education curriculum that also incorporates PST in the teaching of golf to children (Sherman, 1999). Sherman delineated a 5-phase program that encompassed the following psychological dimensions: 1) goal setting (e.g., reminding children about how to hold the club correctly to maximize ball contact, having children set daily goals of their own), 2) attention and concentration (e.g., using cues to reinforce motor skills or for distraction control) 3) imagery training (e.g., mentally rehearsing the motor sequence involved in the golf swing, use of models to reinforce imagery), 4) awareness of elements that affect performance (e.g., tension, fear of failure), and 5) evaluation (e.g., using sensory feedback [how did that swing feel?]). Sherman provided some practical ways of implementing these instructional strategies: teacher commitment, gradual introduction of elements, use of a motor skill that requires lots of motion, hands-on and student-centered, emphasis on the link between the mind and body, use of student journals, and finally, doggedness in pursuing one's goals. This package, as Sherman has suggested, has the potential of providing instruction in positive life skill development that could serve children well into adulthood.

COPING AND YOUTH SPORT

Coping with both external (e.g., parents and coaches) and internal (e.g., unrealistic expectations, performance anxiety, negative thinking) pressures can come with the territory of competing in youth sport. How young athletes cope with these stressors has become an important area of study. As Holt and Mandigo (2004) reported, sport drop-out can be precipitated by anxiety. In fact, drop-out rates can reach as high as 35% (Gould & Petlichkoff as cited in Holt & Mandigo). Essentially, there has been little research on coping in youth sport particularly as related to younger children (see Holt, Hoar, & Fraser, 2005 for an extensive review of youth-related coping literature). According to Holt, Hoar and Fraser, young adolescents and children tend to use social support, detachment, problem solving and isolation as ways of handling stress in sport. Development plays a role in children's use of limited cognitive-based strategies that normally surface in middle adolescence. This does not negate teaching younger children the appropriate competencies through more concrete means. However, more intervention work is required to substantiate the latter claim.

Holt and Mandigo (2004) examined both problem-focused and emotion-focused coping in younger athletes—the former relates to modifying the stressor to reduce anxiety (i.e., focusing on the technical, increasing effort, or practicing), while the latter involves self-regulation strategies used to control arousal levels or emotions through the use of such strategies as negative thought stopping or arousal control. They worked with young, male cricket players (mean age = 11.9), and used concept mapping as the method of gathering data. Using this technique they assessed worries over the short- and long-term, and evaluated how the players dealt with these worries. Qualitative analysis involved identifying emerging themes based on whether the boys drew on problem- or emotion-focused coping responses.

Holt and Mandigo reported that use of the two types of coping strategies were fairly equivalent with thought control the most frequently used emotion-focused strategy (16.93%) and concentration on the technical a commonly used problem solving strategy (29.22%). If coping strategies were linked to major performance worries, problem-focused coping was used over emotion-focused strategies two-thirds of the time. Performance anxiety and negative evaluation by others surfaced as major worries for this cohort—a common finding in the research on stress in youth sport (Holt & Mandigo).

Embracing a transactional model, Anshel and Delany (2001) examined the interdependence between one's appraisal of an event as a positive or negative stressor and resultant ways of coping with the stressors. Self-esteem, cognitive appraisal and perceived control of the stressor are factors that can mediate the interaction between appraisal and coping. Fifty-two field hockey players (36 males and 16 females, aged 10-12) were presented with a list of possible stressors such as making errors, experiencing pain, or being bothered by spectators. Coping strategies were related to competing in their sport. Stressors were defined as situations that really upset, worried, or annoyed the players. Using structured interviews, a checklist and qualitative analysis of the players' responses, participants' assessment of the intensity of game stressors (cognitive appraisal) and resultant coping strategies (approach or avoidance) were examined. Approach coping requires one's taking control of a stressful situation through positive coping strategies while fear anxiety and anger are emotions that can surface through negative appraisals of an event and resultant avoidance behaviors (Anshel & Delany). Avoidance coping may not necessarily be negative according to Anshel and Delany. Often short-term stressors are best dealt with by avoiding them. Dealing with stress is a complex phenomenon.

In Anshel and Delany's (2001) study, content analyses of sources of stress, cognitive appraisals of stressful events, and coping strategies revealed that the most highly rated stressors for both males and females were making errors as well as bad calls by the umpires. Qualitative findings uncovered gender differences in sources of stress however. More negative than positive appraisals of stress surfaced for both genders, and particularly for the girls. Yet, females used more approach strategies than did the males. Avoidance coping was the most frequently cited strategy by the players (e.g., "I tried to forget the whole thing", p. 342). All in all, results revealed that the children avoided perceived negative stressors, and did not back away from what they viewed as positive stressors. It is gratifying that research has been carried out on coping in youth sport. However, as Anshel and Delany suggested, this area of study requires further investigation particularly across different sports, and I may add, age levels. To maintain youth's involvement in sport, knowing what causes stress, burnout, and low self-esteem can only be revealed by exploring the perceptions and psychological skill use of the players themselves.

The underlying message of these studies is that while worries and coping strategies may complement each other, individuals involved in youth sport programs should work toward eliminating the stressors. They also should instill in children the competencies for dealing with the pressure through PST or similar interventions that target emotion-focused skills. It has been well documented that the majority of children participate in sport for fun (e.g., Weiss, 2000; Weiss & Bunker). There also are developmental differences in coping strategies with younger children understanding that effort may lead to enhanced performance (Holt, Hoar, & Fraser, 2005). However, be it competitive or recreational activity, let's leave fun and play in sport and stress out!

In conclusion, future work across different sports, cultures and age groups would expand the somewhat limited knowledge base in the area of psychological skill training and elite or recreational youth participants. There already exists a growing leadership in this field at both the practical and research level. My hope is that this leadership encourages others to pursue opportunities in this greatly neglected area of work. Perhaps, if the concept of life skill development were emphasized, more educators, coaches, and parents would support these attempts, and take a proactive role themselves.

USEFUL RESOURCES

Terry Orlick's book "Free to Feel Great: Teaching Children to Excel at Living" (Orlick, 1993) is an excellent 'how to' PST book that teachers, parents or coaches can use with young children. Support materials include age-appropriate and motivating audio resources designed to reinforce imagery use, stress management, confidence-building and positive self-talk strategies from young children to adult. I have used the book and support material extensively in my classes. They have been extremely well-received by university level students, particularly by student teachers looking for PST-type resources. Orlick has also written numerous books related to games and children. Combining his sport psychology knowledge and understanding of child development, he has been a strong proponent of using mental training for children for both sport and life (Orlick & McCaffrey, 1991). Orlick and McCaffrey have demonstrated that elementary children can be introduced to such mental training skills as relaxation, imagery and concentration through play. The activities are offered to children as fun-oriented games (e.g., progressive muscle relaxation disguised as "spaghetti toes"). Mental training objectives include teaching young children how to take control over their lives, build their self-confidence and enhance their quality of life.

Of practical importance according to Orlick and McCaffrey (1991), is the presence of the following seven conditions when presenting a mental training program to young children: fun, concrete and physical (e.g., place your worries into a tree or worry jar), individualized instruction, multi-modal instructional approaches, optimism, and use of role models. I highly recommend this humanistic approach with children as it also emphasizes self-regulation and other forms of mindfulness. A similar approach to instilling such psychological skills as motivation, self-perceptions, coping and moral development has been embraced by Maureen Weiss in both her research and practical work with children (e.g., Weiss, 1991, 2000; Weiss & Raedeke, 2004).

A source for video material related to sport psychology, Virtual Brands (http://www.vbvideo.com/) has produced "Mental Skills for Young Athletes" (Virtual Brands, 2005). In the program, Dan Gould, well known for his work in sport psychology and Director of the Institute for the Study of Youth Sports at Michigan State University, covers essential psychological skills that can be used with children ages 7-13. Skills include positive thinking, stress management, focusing, and confidence building. Despite the fact that the video primarily uses a 'talking head' approach to instruction, Gould provides excellent examples of practical exercises. This production includes information for coaches and sports psychologists. I would recommend using a section-by-section approach to "Mental Skills for

Young Athletes" where each psychological skill is presented and then discussed in more detail by a facilitator. Older children may also benefit from viewing the video.

REFERENCES

Anshel, M. H., & Delany, J. (2001). Sources of Acute Stress, Cognitive Appraisals, and Coping Strategies Of Male and Female Child Athletes. *Journal of Sport Behavior, 24*(4), 329.

Armstrong, F. D., Collins, F. L., Greene, P., & Panzironi, H. (1988). Effects of Brief Relaxation Training on Children's Motor Functioning. *Journal of Clinical Child Psychology, 17*(4), 310.

Atienza, F. L., Balaguer, I., & Garcia-Merita, M. L. (1998). Video modeling and imaging training on performance of tennis service of 9- to 12-year-old children. *Perceptual & Motor Skills, 87*(2), 518.

Baron, L. J. (1991). Peer tutoring, microcomputer learning and young children. *Journal of Computing in Childhood Education, 2*(4), 27-40.

Baron, L. J. (1998). Tai Chi practice in the elementary classroom. *Canadian Journal of Research in Early Childhood Education, 6*, 341-352.

Baron, L. J., & Faubert, C. (2005). The role of Tai Chi Chuan in reducing state anxiety and enhancing mood of children with special needs. *Journal of Bodywork and Movement Therapies, 9*, 120-133.

Blom, L. C., Hardy, C., J., & Joyner, A. B. (2003). High school athletes' perceptions of sport psychology and preferences for services. *International Sports Journal, 7*(2), 1-12.

Borduin, B. J., Borduin, C. M., & Manley, C. M. (1994). The use of imagery training to improve reading comprehension of second graders. *Journal of Genetic Psychology, 155*(1), 115-118.

Coatsworth, J. D., & Conroy, D. E. (2006). Enhancing the self-esteem of youth swimmers through coach training: Gender and age effects. *Psychology of Sport and Exercise, 7*, 173-192.

Conroy, D. E. D.-C. p. e., & Coatsworth, J. D. (2004). The effects of coach training on fear of failure in youth swimmers: A latent growth curve analysis from a randomized, controlled trial. *Journal of Applied Developmental Psychology, 25*(2), 193.

Danish, S. J. (1996). Learning life skills through sports. *The APA Monitor, 27*(7), 10.

Danish, S. J., & Nellen, V. C. (1997). New roles for sports psychologists: Teaching life skills through sport to at-risk youth. *Quest (Human Kinetics), 49*(1), 100.

Deci, E. L., & Ryan, R. M. (1985). *Intrinsic motivation and self-determination in human behavior.* New York: Plenum Press.

GetPsychedSports.org. Advocating for a written sport psychology curriculum for youth and school sport teams. Retrieved July 10, 2006, from http://www.getpsychedsports.org

Gould, D., Damarjian, N., & Medbery, R. (1999). An examination of mental skills training in junior tennis coaches. *Sport Psychologist, 13*(2), 127-142.

Harrison, P. A., & Narayan, G. (2003). Differences in behavior, psychological factors, and environmental factors associated with participation in school sports and other activities in adolescence. *Journal of School Health, 73*(3), 113-120.

Harwood, C., Middlemas, S., & Reeves, C. (2005). *Mental skills development in elite youth soccer: a coaching behavior intervention programme within a professional soccer academy.* Paper presented at the Conference Name|. Retrieved Access Date|. from URL|.

Harwood, C. G., Cumming, J., & Fletcher, D. (2004). Motivational Profiles and Psychological Skills Use within Elite Youth Sport. *Journal of Applied Sport Psychology, 16*(4), 318-332.

Hinkle, J. S. (1994). Integrating sport psychology and sports counselling: Developmental programming, education, and research. *Journal of Sport Behavior* Retrieved May 16, 2006, from http://search.epnet.com/login.aspx?direct=true&db=aph&an=9605220112

Holt, N. L., Hoar, S., & Fraser, S. N. (2005). How does coping change with development? A review of childhood and adolescence sport coping research. *European Journal of Sport Science, 5*(1), 25-39.

Holt, N. L., & Mandigo, J. L. (2004). Coping with performance worries among youth male cricket players. *Journal of Sport Behavior, 27*(1), 39-57.

Li-Wei, A., Qi-Wei, M., Orlick, T., & Zitzelsberger, L. (1992). The effect of mental imagery training on performance enhancement with 7-10 year-old children. *The Sport Psychologist, 6*, 230-241.

Lohaus, A., Klein-Hebling, J., Vogele, C., & Kuhn-Hennighausen, C. (2001). Psychophysiological effects of relaxation training in children. *British Journal of Health Psychology, 6*, 197-206.

Lohaus, A., & Klein-Hessling, J. (2003). Relaxation in children: Effects of extended and intensified training. *Psychology & Health, 18*(2), 237-249.

Lohaus, A., Klein-Hessling, J., Vogele, C., & Kuhn-Hennighausen, C. (2001). Psychophysiological effects of relaxation training in children. *British Journal of Health Psychology, 6*(2), 197.

Mamassis, G., & Doganis, G. (2004). The effects of a mental training program on juniors pre-competitive anxiety, self-confidence, and tennis performance. *Journal of Applied Sport Psychology, 16*(2), 118-137.

Miller, A., & Donohue, B. (2003). The Development and Controlled Evaluation of Athletic Mental Preparation Strategies in High School Distance Runners. *Journal of Applied Sport Psychology, 15*(4), 321-334.

Nicholls, J. G. (1984). Conceptions of ability and achievement motivation. In R. Ames & C. Ames (Eds.), *Research on motivation in education* (Vol. 1, pp. 39-74). New York: Academic Press.

Norlander, T., Moås, L., & Archer, T. (2005). Noise and stress in primary and secondary school children: Noise reduction and increased concentration ability through a short but regular exercise and relaxation program. *School Effectiveness & School Improvement, 16*(1), 91-99.

Orlick, T. (1993). *Free to feel great : Teaching children to excel at living.* Carp, ON: Creative Bound.

Orlick, T., & McCaffrey, N. (1991). Mental training with children for sport and life. *The Sport Psychologist, 5*, 322-334.

Pain, M. A., & Harwood, C. G. (2004). Knowledge and perceptions of sport psychology within English soccer. *Journal of Sports Sciences, 22*(9), 813-826.

Palmer, S. B., & Wehmeyer, M. L. (2003). Promoting Self-Determination in Early Elementary School. *Remedial & Special Education, 24*(2), 115.

Papacharisis, V. P., Goudas, M., Danish, S. J., & Theodorakis, Y. (2005). The Effectiveness of Teaching a Life Skills Program in a Sport Context. *Journal of Applied Sport Psychology, 17*(3), 247-254.

Sherman, C. P. (1999). Integrating mental management skills into the physical education curriculum. *The Journal of Physical Education, Recreation and Dance, 70*(5), 25-30.

Shilts, M. K., Horowitz, M., & Townsend, M. (2004). an innovative approach to goal setting for adolescents: Guided goal setting. *Journal of Nutrition Education & Behavior, 36*(3), 155-156.

Smith, R. E., & Smoll, F. L. (1997). Coaching the Coaches: Youth Sports as a Scientific and Applied Behavioral Setting. *Current Directions in Psychological Science, 6*(1), 16-21.

Smith, R. E., Smoll, F. L., & Barnett, N. (1995). Reduction of children's sport performance anxiety through social support and stress reduction training for coaches. *Journal of Applied Developmental Psychology, 16*(1).

Smoll, F. L., & Smith, R. E. (2001). Conducting sport psychology training programs for coaches: Cognitive-behavioral principles and techniques. In J. M. Williams (Ed.), *Applied sport psychology: Personal growth to peak performance* (4th ed., pp. 378-400). Mountain View, CA: Mayfield Publishing Co.

Speilberger, C. D., Edwards, C. D., Montuori, J., & Lushene, R. (1970). STAIC C-2 Preliminary Manual. Palo Alto, CA: Consulting Psychologists Press.

Virtual Brands. (2005). Mental skills for young athletes. Wibraham, MA.

Weiss, M. R. (1991). Psychological skill development in children and adolescents. *The Sport Psychologist, 5*, 335-354.

Weiss, M. R. (2000). Motivating kids in physical activity. *The President's Council on Physical Fitness and Sports Research Digest, Series 3*(11), 1-8.

Weiss, M. R., & Bunker, L. K. Coaching children to embrace a "love of the game". Retrieved May 26, 2006, from http://www.sirc.ca/

Weiss, M. R., & Raedeke, T. D. (2004). Developmental sport and exercise psychology: Research status on youth and directions toward a lifespan perspective. In M. R. Weiss (Ed.), *Developmental sport and exercise psychology: A lifespan approach* (pp. 1-26). Morgantown, WV: Fitness Information Technology.

Wilson, P. H., Thomas, P. R., & Maruff, P. (2002). Motor Imagery Training Ameliorates Motor Clumsiness in Children. *Journal of Child Neurology, 17*(7), 491.

World Health Organization. (1999). *Partners in life skills education.* Geneva, Switzerland: World Health Organization.

Chapter 5

THE COMMERCIAL SIDE OF SPORT

As you wander through a park or school grounds, it is likely that you will notice that the majority of children are sporting caps and T-shirts with either the Nike 'swish' or Adidas stripes, a cartoon hero, or a favorite team logo. In addition, there may be a prevalence of youth wearing jerseys, sweaters and jackets branded or died in the colors of various sports teams or sport-related brands or companies. Often on the back of these jerseys are the names of their favorite hockey, basketball or football hero. You also might notice at your child's hockey practice that many of the players are wearing Reebok skates, the skate worn by many a National Hockey League (NHL) star including young phenom Sidney Crosby who has become a marketable commodity for the NHL as Michael Jordan was for Nike and the NBA. Professional sport leagues even have licensing agreements with furniture manufacturers as a means of targeting the growing market of children and teenagers both as a fan base and as future consumers (Jensen, 1996). From appealing images, role models, giveaways and promotional items, children of all ages are exposed to the business side of sport, and more often than not, they and their parents are unaware of their place in a broader marketing scheme designed to transform them into unrestrained consumers of the bountiful by-products of sport.

Questions arise as to why sport has emerged from the playing field or arena into the lives of our youth in such an pervasive way, and what impact this has had on their values, beliefs and consumer behavior? How has sport marketing become such an influence within our society that the culture of sport reaches beyond appreciating the level of skill to a space that reflects the values and beliefs that the marketers would like us to identify with? Are there answers in psychology and sociology literature to explain such a phenomenon, or has the knowledge been restricted to the purview of those in advertising and marketing who have described the phenomenon as an 'exchange process' (Jackson, 2000)? The latter concept refers to the marketing of sport products and services to the consumer and consumer products and services through sport.

Historically, as Slack (1998) pointed out, even Greek athletes were financially compensated for their efforts in the early Olympics (B.C.E). However, as he also stressed, there has been a precedent-setting increase in the commercialization of sport during the last two decades. Whether the average person is aware of it or not, sport has become big business and business is involved in sport. Amateur or professional, sport is now heavily combined with marketing schemes such as licensing agreements and merchandising. Athletes of all ages, sports organizations and teams are viewed as marketable commodities in an ever-growing marketplace. Even parents are responsible for the trend by promoting their children through contracts with large sports brands. For example, it has been reported that the parents of a three-year-old child sent a video of their son making 18 baskets in a row to Reebok (Mravic & Deitsch, 2003). The company signed him to a promotional contract that included a college trust fund to be secured in 2018.

Citing the literature on developmental differences, Pine and Nash (2005) underscored the fact that young children "have higher trust, lower recall and lower understanding of commercial messages than older children" (p. 7). They do not necessarily have the cognitive capabilities to understand persuasive intent, which requires perspective taking ability despite the fact that they can distinguish programming from commercials (Acuff as cited in Pine & Nash, 2003; Oates, Blades & Gunter, 2002, Pine & Nash, 2005). Child-brand relationships develop early in life. Research in consumer behavior already has shown that children under age 8 are the most susceptible to advertising and marketing schemes while children as young as age 2 show brand reliance (Hite & Hite, 1995).

Children can be heavy consumers themselves, and strongly influence family spending (the 'nag' factor). Furham (as cited in Oates, Blades, & Gunter, 2002) reported that U.S. children, ages 4 -12, spent over 24 billion dollars, and influenced family spending to the order of 190 billion dollars. In 2004, 3.7 billion dollars were spent on children's athletic shoes and 8.1 billion on children's sports apparel in the U.S. (SGMA International's Sports Apparel & Athletic Footwear Market Facts and Trends 2005 edition. SGMA International, accessed May 30, 05, http://www.sgma.com/press/2005/press1109693939-10466.html; email June 1, 2005 from Mike May of SGMA Int'l). This amount was up 12.1% from the previous year! Billions of dollars are spent annually in sport marketing, and billions are spent by families who purchase clothing, equipment, shoes, caps, etc. that carry popular brand logos or the names of sport heroes. Essentially, children have become walking billboards, and free advertising for the corporate world of sport.

There is a large body of research in advertising and consumer behavior as related to sport marketing. As well, the general literature on children as consumers is fairly comprehensive although not necessarily in the social science literature. Various themes have emerged from the world of commerce. Besides well-known marketing tactics, product endorsements, utilizing athletes as role models, using sport to sell non-sport-related products, and developing life-long brand awareness are key features of sport marketing.

An essential goal of this chapter is to enlighten parents, coaches, teachers and children about advertising conventions and marketing concepts with the goal of educating them about how to make more critical judgments about the effects of sport marketing on youth as well as how to become more wise consumers themselves.

PRODUCT ENDORSEMENTS

In describing David Beckham's launching of an Adidas soccer boot, editors of the *Montreal Gazette* (June 2, 2005) put a spin on a well-known movie title by using the headline "brand it like Beckham" on its cover banner. If the advertisement had depicted an average Joe or Jane wearing this shoe, in this competitive age of sports apparel, it would be highly unlikely that it would become popular or command the high price tag.

An excellent example of athletes' loyalty through product endorsements was provided by Wenner (1994). He recalled the experience of some USA basketball 'Dream Team' players refusing to wear the official shoe of the 1992 summer Olympics because of their endorsement contracts with other companies. Members of the team who had been contracted by Nike at the time covered the Reebok logo on their tracksuits as they stood on the podium to receive their medals. This experience personifies the extent to which athletes, both amateur and professional, have contracted themselves out to endorse not only athletic footwear and apparel, but also consumer products of all kinds (e.g., the George Foreman grill). There are those from the world of sport who have expressed fear that the Olympics and other world sporting events have moved away from the ideals of amateur sport by becoming over-commercialized with cross-merchandising and advertising agreements. Competition for huge television contracts for major sporting events has become the norm. Unendorsed sponsors have been reduced to "ambush" (p. 28) or "parasitic" (p.29) marketing strategies by placing their advertisements near those endorsed by the Olympics (Wenner). In the consumer's mind, the Olympic movement and amateur sport have always symbolized the highest ideals of fairplay and sport. Marketers have taken advantage of this association in advertising their products or setting up sponsorship contracts. As is the case with all advertising, the consumer, child or adult, must become aware of advertisers' game plans. If fans are directly addressed or seen as part of the "community" portrayed in the promotions, the effect can be even more pronounced (Wenner). Recall the very successful 1980 Super Bowl commercial by Coca Cola (Mean Joe Green Super Bowl Ad, July 4, 05: http://progressive.stream.aol.com/aol/us/specials/2004/superbowl/spots_web/coke_meanjoe_dl.mov). The ad portrayed Joe Green taking a bottle of Coca Cola from a young fan, and in return, giving him his football jersey. The message being conveyed was that Coke 'added life' to this youth's day by addressing the needs of "the reader" (Wenner, p. 30). Wenner described the process as both the readers' and advertisers' constructing the meanings of some commercials by bringing "sports dirt" (p. 29) into them. Wenner depicted the 'reading' of advertisements as a form of negotiation between the meanings the advertisers intend to convey and the meanings the viewer constructs. Successful commercials also have been shown to play with one's emotions while promoting the product. Unfortunately, those in the health promotion field have under-utilized similarly effective advertisements conventions. Unfortunately, the public sector simply cannot compete with the private sector in compensating athletes.

ATHLETES AS ROLE MODELS

Athletes who have earned the status of role model often are used to endorse and sell products. As already discussed in this chapter, the athlete (amateur or professional) is very much a part of the sport marketing plan to the point where athletes on the international stage have become symbols of the corporate world more so than of their own countries. Youth identify strongly with their sport heroes, and promoters use this relationship to sell both sports and products. Research (Steinberg & Tkacik, 2003) even has shown that consumers are not bothered by athletes who have encountered legal problems (e.g., Kobe Bryant who was accused of sexual assault). Role models shown wearing, playing with or using product brands legitimizes product use in the minds of the unenlightened consumer. Commercials that show the foibles of sports heroes have been shown to be particularly effective (Wenner, 1994). In these advertisements, consumers gain supposed insights into their sport heroes' weaknesses which makes them human, more like us, and even more effective as role models--"We know Dave. We like Dave. Be like Dave. Buy the Corn Flakes to get the jacket" (Wenner, p. 39).

Advertisements also are designed to place the consumer in the ad through surrogate figures that the 'reader' can identify with (e.g., child; parent; teacher; fun-loving, beer drinking young adults). Identification with main and secondary characters; appeals to cultural ideals; beliefs and desires such as patriotism, multiculturalism, teamwork, sports participation and social mobility; and the power of sports heroes are designed to motivate the consumer to be like them (Wenner, 1994). In attempts to mirror the consumer, role models motivate the latter to buy shoes, clothing, trading cards, electrical appliances, cars, athletic equipment, sports drinks, and so forth. Unfortunately, as Wenner suggested, the consumer generally knows little about their sports hero beyond his or her competitive proficiency in the sporting arena. The public constructs (or is led to construct) an incomplete impression of the athlete, creating a 'hero' in all aspect of life. Marketers take advantage of these perceptions.

Another issue is whether and how much a child's sense of identity, values and norms are influenced by what images they see through media. For example, if the media's coverage of women's sport or advertising images perpetuate stereotypical gender roles of women athletes as sex objects or more generally under represent female athletes (Cuneen & Sidwell, 1998; Shugart, 2003), what message is being conveyed to young girls? In fact, women present a larger percentage of the fitness market than men, and more recently, sporting goods companies have made attempts to project women as strong and athletic (Cuneen & Sidwell). Research should address whether this trend in changing advertising images will continue across what is considered a male-dominated industry and how, in the long-term, these representations of women impact on the roles and values inculcated by children.

Using Social Learning Theory (modeling) as the theoretical basis for much of the research, media's influence on, for example, body image and satisfaction, aggression, fashion and smoking has been thoroughly examined. As Taveres et al. (2004) pointed out, there has been a paucity of work on the media's influence on healthy behaviors like active living or sport participation. Significant others, whether peers, parents, teachers or media figures, have the potential of influencing children's involvement in physical activity and sport through identification with these role models.

In a USA study of close to 17,000 (ages 9 – 16), girls (46%) appeared to be more influenced than boys (27%) by media figures they were exposed to on television, movies and magazines (Taveres et al., 2004). Studying the determinants of adolescent physical activity, Taveres et al. correlated the influence of modeling with physical activity levels, and discovered a positive correlation between the two variables particularly with older participants. In other words, the more youth stated wanting to emulate media figures, the more physically active they reported being. Tavares et al. stated that the differences in physical activity levels between those who wanted to look "totally" (one of the response intervals in the scale) like media figures versus those who did not was approximately 3.5 hours of additional physical activity per week for girls and 6 hours per week for boys! They controlled for such factors as parental influence and personal and social factors (e.g., body satisfaction, self esteem, peer influences). This data aligns with previous work correlating the relationship between exposure to sport media and physical activity. Although assessed, the researchers did not discuss how television-viewing habits factored into the results. One cannot assume from their research that the amount of media exposure alone motivated the participants to look like media figures and therefore physical activity levels. In fact, research has convincingly uncovered negative correlations between television-viewing and being active. While much has been said about the negative influence of media role models on youth, what stands out in their work is Tavare's et al.'s uncovering a positive relationship between identification with media figures and physical activity. There is obviously potential for various media to project positive and healthy lifestyle habits to children and adolescents.

Constructive use of the media is the 'good news'. Now... for the 'bad news' (depending on your perspective of course). If media has the ability of being a positive social influence as demonstrated by Tavares' group, what other role does mass media play in influencing young consumers? More specifically, how do role models such as athletes (i.e., those who have no direct contact with individuals) vicariously influence youth's purchasing decisions (and indirectly their 'pester power')? Martin and Bush (2000) examined the question with adolescents whom they reported as spending nearly US$100 billion a year (as cited in Zollo, 1995). They identified teenagers as an influential marketing target--the trend setters for the larger population. Martin and Bush hypothesized that the influence of role models and adolescents' purchasing intentions would be linked. Amongst other social influences such as parents, peers and movie stars, they teased out the effects of well-known athletes as "consumption role models" (p. 443). Their supposition was that vicarious role models are chosen by youth, and are therefore very compelling. These role models tend to be of the same sex and race. Martin and Bush examined whether parents, as direct role models, influenced adolescents purchasing intentions and behavior more than what they called indirect role models (e.g., athletes). They used a role model influence scale (e.g., identify your "favorite" [p. 446] athlete) and a purchase intentions and behavior scale (e.g., The opinions of my [father, mother, favorite entertainer or favorite athlete] influence me to recommend products or brands to someone who seeks my advice, Martin & Bush, p. 451) to test their hypotheses with 218 adolescents (ages 13-18). All role models were significant predictors of purchasing intentions. The researchers expressed surprise at the significant relationships between purchasing intentions and entertainers and athletes. The results are not surprising, however, considering existing knowledge about the influence of mass media, including sports as entertainment, on youth. Comparing role models, entertainers and athletes did not have as direct an influence on adolescents' purchasing intentions and behavior as did fathers and mothers. Analyzing mean influence, the researchers revealed that mothers had a greater influence than fathers while athletes outdid favorite entertainers. These findings were of use to marketers. The researchers proposed that advertising executives use the results in marketing campaigns (e.g., in particular, be conscious of not offending parents and particularly those of pre- or early adolescence). Indeed, the findings are also informative to parents, educators and coaches whose responsibilities may include enlightening youth about the motivations behind the use of recognized 'stars' to sell products. Parents in particular should also be made aware of their unspecified role as purveyors of consumerism or pawns of the marketing world.

Sport marketing also involves using interest in sports to serve the needs of marketers by providing venues for advertising. As demonstrated in the following study, as consumers, young people are not immune to such schemes. Analyzing *Sports Illustrated for Kids (SIK)* whose median age of readership is 11/12 years old, Cuneen and Sidwell (1998) investigated gender-role portrayals. SIK attracts a readership of 8.1 million readers a month (June 27, 05; http://www.sikids.com/magmediakit/franchise/mag_fran.htm). The magazine with accompanying teacher's guide is also distributed to 8,000 classrooms (200,000 children) in disadvantaged areas as part of a U.S-based literacy program. Readership data for 2000 has indicated that the ratio of male to female readers was 69%:31% and subscribers to non-subscribers, 82%:18% (June 27, 05; http://www.sikids.com/magmediakit/reader/mag_reader.htm). SIK's contribution to the area of literacy should be acknowledged and applauded. However, it should not go unnoticed that this magazine, specifically targeted to youth, serves advertisers' needs as well.

In their study, Cuneen and Sidwell (1998) carried out a content analysis of the advertising images in *SIK* with the underlying belief that that the images may serve as significant gender socialization agents in children's lives—influencing values and beliefs including consumer behavior. Surveys had already established the influence of *SIK* advertisements on the purchase of sports shoes, clothing, toys, and other consumer items. Coders were instructed to record the content of the advertisements in *SIK* in terms of who were the prominent and supporting models, whether the latter were represented in team or individual activities, and what recreational activities were represented. Coders also noted the gender and product categories represented by the ads. One might assume that the researchers were investigating what the marketers already knew. The results of the content analysis revealed that males were more prominent models in all activities (a 12:1 ratio of male: female). As supportive models, with the exception of combined sport/recreational and individual sports, males again were depicted more often than females (6:1). Males outnumbered females in product categories (e.g., equipment/clothing, sports products) both as prominent and supporting models. It is not surprising that the researchers not only uncovered stereotypical portrayals of males and females, but also that males predominated the magazine's advertisements. Boys also were depicted as more actively engaged while females served as spectators and supporters (e.g., a mother cheering on a child athlete [usually male]). The target audience for *SIK* is predominantly male, and the advertisers justifiably market to them. However, the publishers have committed to a literacy program in schools, and should present a balanced gender perspective. In examining www.SIKIDS.COM (June 27, 05; http://www.sikids.com/), the images and headings were all male-oriented. Over a year later, this had not changed! Also, the editorial calendar identified male professional leagues (e.g., NBA, NHL, NFL) as its 2005 highlights. While SIK has committed to a school-based program, one may aptly question the true motives behind involvement in such a program when its advertisements, and more recently its website, continue to perpetuate stereotypical views of males and females. Is the bottom line profit or true commitment to literacy? What kind of social statements are magazines and websites like *SIK* making to youth in perpetuating gender stereotypes about sports participants? With its extensive circulation to both youth and adults, *SIK* could play a pivotal role in "portraying the genders in coequal roles" (Cuneen & Sidwell). After all, even women's football has become a popular spectator sport despite the fact that procuring television exposure, including advertising, is difficult (Fitzgerald, 2003). In fact, since 2002, the NFL has taken advantage of women as a growing audience (40%) by partnering with Reebok to make fan apparel for women (Fitzgerald, 2003). As Gardyn (2001) stated, "they may throw like girls, but young female sports fans (ages 9 - 13) present a 'Super Bowl' of an opportunity for marketers" (p. 12). In fact, as Gardyn reported, the Internet has opened up new sport marketing avenues targeted at young girls who are both heavy users and technologically literate. Fitzgerald also mentioned the NFL's marketing plan, which includes the development of videogames to attract youth-- future fans and consumers. The lines between sport, entertainment and business no doubt have become blurred.

With changing perceptions of women in sport over the last decade, perhaps it would be more appropriate to conduct content analyses of "girl-oriented" magazines in terms of portrayals of active females. Have the images changed in the last decade or two? In the meantime, significant people in children's lives (including community sports organizations) have the opportunity of instilling in both boys and girls a gender inclusive vision of youth sports (Baron & Downey, submitted for review). Doing so might help to heighten all children's perceptions that they are capable of and can perform in any sport at any level if the models they are exposed to through significant others and the media convey to them this message.

SPORT AS A MARKETING MEDIUM

Schooler and Feighery (1996) reported that in 1993 the tobacco industry spent almost $162 million on sporting events and public entertainment. Sport sponsorship in general reached $4.55 billion by 1998 (Kuzma, Veltri, Kuzma, & Miller, 2003). Sponsorship from the naming of arenas and stadiums and subsidizing sporting events is now common practice. High schools have begun to follow the trend of colleges and universities as product brands (including sports-related, doughnut and tire companies) have acquired naming rights to gyms and sports centers, sport events, baselines, jump circles and ticket stubs (Pennington, 2004). One would be naive to believe that companies finance events solely for the good of sport. As seen in Schooler and Feighery's (1996) work, advertising at sport venues has an impact on the consumer. Performance Research, a marketing analysis firm specializing in sport sponsorship, cites as its philosophy, "We view sponsorship as offering something more meaningful, more emotional, and more lasting than simple advertising. It's about "passion, relevancy, loyalty, and return-on-relationship" (http://www.performanceresearch.com/philosophy.htm; accessed June 16, 05). From golf, NASCAR and Formula One racing, tennis, skiing, aqua events and other spectator sports, the corporate world is there vying for the consumer dollar.

Slack (1998) presented a provocative perspective of the commercialism of sport from a sociological viewpoint. He described sport marketing as creating commodities not only of children and sport organizations, but also of the products of sports including athletes, logos, and sportswear. He suggested that reductions in government funding for amateur sport has created a void easily filled by the private sector where participants are beholden to both their organization (the recipient of funding) and the corporate sponsor. For example, in the attempt to attract sponsors, representatives of the Canada Games Council state on their website that, "the Canada Games is the ideal partner to help you leverage your brand while gaining tremendous local, regional and national exposure in connection with this strong Canadian tradition... the Canada Games offers an expansive list of sponsor benefits to customize a fully integrated package that fits your marketing objectives." (http://www.canadagames.ca/Content/Organization/Marketing.asp?langid=1; June 14/05). Cited are such benefits as television exposure, PR campaigns and an affiliation with this high profile movement. There are numerous sport marketing programs offered at the university level. From a marketing perspective, the phenomenon is a win-win situation. The sponsor is provided with exposure; the amateur athlete financial support. However, from a sociological perspective, Slack refers to this relationship as one of power in which the sponsor is the possessor and the mediator of the relationship and the athlete a pawn in a larger marketing plan. As Slack described, and as mentioned earlier in the chapter, world-class athletes perform for companies and not necessarily for their own country (e.g., "the Speedo athletes" [http://www.speedo.com/; accessed June 16,05]). Is it a win-win situation when sports networks like ESPN and US Magazine promote "the world's sexiest athletes"?

In 1999, the NFL blitzed the youth market in order to attract the next generation fan to the game of football (Jensen, 1998). With star athletes endorsing the 'product' (i.e., the game itself) and partnerships with Quaker Oats, Nike, Gatorade, Hasbro (NFL Monopoly game and NFL handbook for children), Kmart and Ford, the NFL set a plan in motion. Other sport leagues have implemented similar marketing strategies in an attempt to entice youth. This approach is somewhat the flipside of using sport to sell products. That is, this strategy involves making use of non sport-related products to sell sport.

DEVELOPING BRAND AWARENESS

There are different perspectives to exploring the development of the child as consumer. Developmental approaches provide a very useful framework in which to examine both children's understanding of marketing as well as their behavior as consumers. However, due to the paucity of pertinent developmental work in the sport domain, implications must be extrapolated from the larger research literature.

McNeal (as cited in Davis, 2004) described the child as one who, (1) buys, (2) influences others to buy, and (3) develops a lifelong brand loyalty as s/he develops into an adult consumer. Advertisers take full advantage of all three characteristics. Establishing a 'brand personality' in future consumers is part of the building blocks model (Davis, 2004). Marketing is designed not only to make a consumer feel good about themselves, but to establish brand loyalty. To influence consumers, products are portrayed as exciting, trendy, and fun. These brand 'personalities' help to develop strong relationships between the consumer and product. Advertisers are well-versed in how to sell their products based on the cognitive, affective and behavioral development of children. From a marketing perspective, life-long brand loyalty is crucial. The relationship between consumer and product starts when a young child is first introduced to advertising, and can extend into adulthood. In fact, as pointed out by Davis, early studies (1944 and 1964) reported that almost one-quarter of childhood brand choices carry into adulthood! From a marketer's perspective, it seems reasonable to target children as consumers, and to develop what becomes an enduring childhood-friendship relationship between child and product early in a child's life (Fournier as cited in Davis).

Ji (2001) developed the MOA framework to describe how child-brand relationships develop. All the elements are in place if the brand helps build self-esteem (M = motivation), opportunities (O) for the child to interact with the brand are increased, and the child has developed the cognitive, emotional and behavioral (i.e., can ask for or buy a product) abilities (A) to form such a relationship. The marketer's role is to create a 'nostalgic relationship' between the consumer and particular product (Fournier as cited in Davis, 2004), and to imprint and strengthen this relationship through advertising. Advertising is designed to appeal particularly to the cognitive and emotional modalities of individual consumers. The main concern with respect to young children is that their cognitive and emotional schema are not very sophisticated. Bombarded through different medium including television, computers, videogames, films, toys, clothes, peers and parents, a child can hardly avoid the constant barrage of advertised messages the intent of which a very young child may not be aware. The lack of advertising literacy (and we adults are not great at it either!) can lead to children's nagging their parents for particular products and brands.

Oates, Blades and Gunter (2002) reported that children between 6 and 14 years watch approximately 20,000 TV commercials a year in the United States and 18,000 in the UK. Underscoring the power of advertising, Schooler and Feighery (1996) examined the relationship between cigarette marketing through various media and the smoking behavior and consumer behavior of an ethnically diverse and disadvantaged sample of adolescents. They found that those who reported more exposure to advertising were both more likely to smoke and own cigarette-related promotional items. Gender differences also mediated the findings with boys more cognizant of cigarette advertising, including those on billboards and at sporting events, and twice as likely to have experimented with cigarettes than girls. Developing brand equity (i.e., intrinsic value of the product for the consumer) and brand value (i.e., making products meaningful in the mind of consumers) are primary goals of marketers. As one would expect, brand awareness and brand loyalty strengthen throughout development. If, through advertising, consumers indelibly store brand labels in their cognitive database, and are able to retrieve them easily (i.e., brand recall), the marketers have done their job well. As well, marketing and brand identification through the medium of television has been shown to have a powerful influence on preschoolers (Macklin, 1996; Pine & Nash, 2003). Even young children can learn and recall brand names. Macklin's goal was to examine how children learn brand names from visual cues.

Using developmental theory as the basis of her three studies, Macklin (1996) investigated whether, how many and what type of visual cues (e.g., color, pictures) enhanced preschoolers learning of brand names (none were sport-related). As expected, there were developmental differences in recall scores between preschoolers and seven- and eight-year olds. Both groups, however, learned brand names better when the visual packaging of products was meaningful to them and when associated cues (e.g., grass and green, or night and stars) were used in the packaging. Too many visual cues proved detrimental to young children's learning. This should be expected considering eye movement studies with young children (Baron, 1980). No gender differences surfaced in Macklin's studies. In order to counteract the power of marketing, parents, teachers, and coaches should be responsible for instilling in children an understanding of how advertising is designed to attract attention to and enhance the encoding and retrieval of brand names. Appeals to the perceptual and emotional are two strategies that advertisers effectively use.

In her Australian-based study, Davis (2004) interviewed 26 children (ages 5 - 12; 12 boys and 14 girls). Developmental in nature, she examined how child-brand interactions become child-brand relationships. Taking an ecological approach, media, family and peers were also factored into the analysis in order to evaluate their influence. Similar to most research in this area, her investigation was to uncover information for the use of marketers. However, the findings naturally are useful to those individuals who would like to heighten children's advertising literacy in order to make them less susceptible to advertising schemes. Children were asked about their feelings for particular brand products. Davis then analyzed the transcripts from these unstructured interviews, and looked for common themes in the participants' responses. The analyses were designed to examine whether children's interactions with particular products could in fact be considered as 'relationships' that would have lifelong viability. Using interpersonal relationship theory as a basis for her investigation, Davis examined the effects of product or people cues on brand recall and retrieval. Memory of brands indicated that a 'relationship' did indeed exist between child and product. Davis also assessed whether there was an emotional tie between the two (a critical variable in establishing person-product relationships in marketing). Her results demonstrated that all 26 children had indeed established relationships with particular brands. Davis cited an example of an eight-year-old child who recalled her initial experiences with a particular brand at age two! The product obviously had been registered deeply in her memory. She also reported that the majority of children verbalized feelings toward particular brands (e.g., It makes me feel nice when referring to a particular brand of yogurt or It makes my hair all fruity smelling and I feel like I did a good thing- it makes me feel like a good girl!). She emphasized that adults, particularly parents, initiate these child-brand relationships. Studying family effects, she found that children of divorce as well as remarried parents increased the number of brand interactions as did birth order (older siblings influenced younger children), gender (girls were more aware of toiletries than snacks) and number of siblings. In other studies, viewing alone led to requests for more products from Santa Claus, and various media, including children's magazines appeared to have a cognitive as well as emotional influence on brand relationships (e.g., the puppy is so cute in the tissue ad). The effects of television exposure to brand items have been well documented (Pine & Nash, 2005).

Children also cited peers as sources for brand information (Davis, 2005). Peers are a major influence in consumer purchasing particularly for adolescents. Davis mentioned sharing lunches (brand swapping) and sleepovers as opportunities for peers to expose each other to various brands. She used the metaphor 'arranged marriages' to describe how children are introduced to particular brands through significant others. The latter play a considerable role in initiating youngsters to sport-related brands and products through their own emotional ties. Marketers and advertisers have positioned and promoted their products well if these child-brand marriages have emanated from the memory and emotional links that others have. For example, what brand baseball glove or bat do you remember being introduced to by your parents? Have you perpetuated their choices as a parent? Besides brand swapping, Davis described other strategies used by marketers and advertisers as means of reinforcing child-brand relationships and sport-related consumerism. These conventions include, monogamy (loyalty to a brand), trophy brands (the brand is 'cool' or 'in'), secret desire (you want it because you cannot have it), and addiction/dependency (satisfying a need for comfort beyond what is considered healthy).

In a study carried out in the United Kingdom that directly investigated the relationship between young children's brand choices and the power of advertising. Pine and Nash (2003) examined whether, if given a choice, preschoolers preferred brands offered on television to non-advertised more generic products. The participants were children who watched an average of 2.5 hours of television a day, of which only 1.4% of their waking time was spent watching advertisements. Pine and Nash created a scenario designed to ask 75 children (38 boys and 37 girls), ages 4 - 5, what foods, candies, toys, and so forth the experimenter should bring to their house for a guest the child's age. They asked children to choose items by pointing to photographs of either well-known brands or identical, non-advertised products. Pine and Nash hypothesized that the choices children made, regularly advertised versus non-advertised items, would demonstrate the effects of televised advertising. Branded items included a drink, toy, chocolate bar, breakfast cereal, sneakers (Nike) and T-shirt (Adidas). The researchers noted that the sportswear was advertised during regular early and late evening programs, and not during children's programs. Of 600 possible choices, children overwhelmingly picked the branded products (406 or 67.67%) over the non-branded (194 or 32.33%) products demonstrating that even young children can be influenced by televised advertising. Interesting gender and product differences surfaced. Girls chose more advertised products than boys as well as branded over non-branded products (particularly the cereal) with the exception of the sneakers. Gender differences also surfaced by product category. Girls significantly chose the well-known product in all categories except the sneakers and T-shirt while significant differences for boys' choices surfaced only for the cereal and the T-shirt. Pine and Nash cited gender socialization (i.e., the idea that females are the "shoppers", and girls tend to accompany their mothers shopping where they are exposed to food products), viewing habits, differences in verbal ability (i.e., developing brand preferences requires linguistic processing skills) and emotional sensitivity (i.e., more susceptible to emotional appeals by the advertisers) as possible explanations for the gender differences. The findings are somewhat unexpected; particularly for the Nike sneakers considering the wide exposure of this brand. One possible explanation is that young children recognize brands that are considered more important to them such as 'munchies' and toys, and only become aware of adult-oriented products as they mature and differentiate different brands and their classifications (Roedder John, 1999). A similar phenomenon was illustrated in Achenreiner's work (as cited in Roedder John).

Given a choice between Nike and Kmart sneakers, second graders showed no preferences while sixth graders and older children chose the 'cooler' or more popular Nike. Achenreiner attributed the findings to developmental underpinnings related to socialization. In time, children grasp the meanings of cues through mass media, family members, and peers as to the presumed status value of products and brand names. Underscoring the importance of being accepted by the 'in crowd', Achenreiner quoted an 11-year-old as saying, "I wear what I wear because it is in style... it also makes me feel real cool... . Clothes I like are Nike, Guess, Levi's and Reebok. I also blend in with all the other people at school and everywhere else I go" (as cited in Roedder John, p. 194).

Suggesting that children become consumers at a very young age, Pine and Nash (2005) analyzed preschoolers' letters to Santa Claus, and correlated their requests with television viewing behavior. Those who watched more commercial television requested more items, However, while asking for the most advertised brands, oddly enough, the children did not request those toys specifically promoted before Christmas. The researchers suggested that those younger than 7 years old had little brand recall skills or, at the very least, were not immediately influenced by a bombardment of television commercials.

Advertisers extensively have promoted products beyond the medium of television through the internet, popular figures (animated or live), billboards, clothing and personal accessories just to mention of few of the means by which their messages are conveyed. Children are bombarded by brand names through practically all of their senses including their emotions! These multi-sensory appeals commensurately increase the strength of brand identification with the effect being more pronounced for young children whose level of critical thinking is not sophisticated despite the fact that studies have shown that they understand the difference between advertisements and programming on television (Hite & Hite, 1995; Levin, Petros, & Petrella, 1982). In fact, Hite and Hite suggested that brand awareness is already developed in toddlers of 2 years. Despite these findings, research also has shown that even children age 10 do not fully comprehend the persuasive intent, bias, and deception in advertising, and do not fully comprehend the nature of additional advertising "tactics" (e.g., use of music, visual cues, celebrity endorsers) and appeals until early adolescence (Oates, Blades, & Gunter, 2002). One of my goals in writing this chapter is to heighten awareness in adults who, in turn, influence youth. Diverse findings related to the influence of advertising on young children's cognitions and behavior leave the door open to further developmental research that would serve both parents and children well.

INTERVENTIONS

As a means of protecting children from televised advertisements, Sweden and other countries (e.g., Australia, Norway and Greece) have either instituted a ban on television advertising to children less than age 12, or have banned toy ads after 10 p.m. (Oates, Blades, & Gunter, 2002). In Canada, Advertising Standards Canada Children's Clearance Committee made up of advertisers, broadcasters, regulators, parents and educators, evaluates televised advertising to children using the Canadian Broadcast Code criteria of developmental appropriateness (http://www.cca-canada.com/ethics/, May 30, 2005, Responsibility and Children's Advertising, Concerned Children's Advertisers). Advertisements that do not meet this code are rejected. Notably, a proposal by the Federal Trade Commission in the U.S. to prohibit televised advertising to children younger than age eight was defeated in 1978.

At first glance a restrictive policy seems worthwhile, however, how effective are such bans with satellite reception, internet, and other means of reaching youth if adults fail to establish controls? One effective mode of counteracting the effects of advertising is the consumer education role that parents and educators can play. Parents, in particular, would be wise to discuss the conventions and motives of advertising with their children while teachers should introduce the topic through media literacy lessons. A similar initiative with university students proved very positive from a consumer perspective with students developing a more critical opinion of Nike's sponsorship of university level sports (Kuzma, Veltri, Kuzma, & Miller, 2003). A developmentally appropriate curriculum would be equally effective with children. It is a marketer's mission to insure that early development of brand awareness carries over into later childhood, adolescents and adulthood. Marketers work to insure that the relationship between a brand and the individual is seen as a long-term one. To counteract the knowledge marketers and advertisers use to establish the 'marriage' between a child and a particular brand requires education of significant others about the development their own brand relationships as well as tools for instilling in children literacy about the world of marketing and consumerism.

CONCLUSION... MARKETERS KNOW BEST?

For some reason, those concerned about the welfare of children have not been the primary parties closely involved in research on the effects of advertising on youth. The lion's share of knowledge seems to be in the purview of those in the marketing community who use this knowledge to sell products. Most of the research and theory reviewed in this chapter has evolved through the research efforts of the latter. In fact, Roedder John (1999) provided one of the most extensive reviews of research on children as consumers using work reported by "consumer researchers" (p. 184) that was published in "marketing and communication journals" (p. 184). Focusing primarily on consumer socialization and albeit, using a developmental backdrop to her discussion, Roedder John admitted excluding research by psychologists, public health and medical researchers in her review. The lack of research from the social scientists indicates a sad state of affairs from the perspective of parents, youth and educators. Available research on marketing and consumer behavior needs to be transformed into practical applications. As Pine and Nash (2003) stated, "there is still a lack of research aimed at determining the extent to which young children (preschoolers) are aware of, or affected by, this constant exposure to commercial persuasion" (p. 1). One must keep in mind that this persuasion, as mentioned previously, is limited not only to television advertising, but encompasses all forms of media including the computer.

Finally from what the literature has uncovered about advertising and children, the following practical suggestions are made for parents and educators:

1. Parents... Watch television with your child, and highlight the differences between reality and fantasy, fact and fiction.
2. Discuss advertising conventions such as persuasive intent, the development of brand awareness, emotional need, and advertisers' motives.
3. Compare different brands and products with children. Discuss why the generic, less expensive brand may be as good if not better than the highly advertised one or the one their peers are wearing.
4. Reduce the amount of commercial television viewing in your home and you'll reduce "pester power" (Pine & Nash, 2005) for brand products.
5. Websites often gather information about children for the purpose of marketing. Set up filtering software on your home computers.

REFERENCES

Baron, L. (1980). The interaction between television and child-related characteristics as demonstrated by eye-movement research. *Educational Communications and Technology: A Journal of Theory, Research. and Development, 28,* 267 - 281.

Baron, L., & Downey, P. (Submitted for review). Children's perceptions of success and fun in physical education.

Cuneen, J., & Sidwell, J. (1998). Gender portrayals in Sports Illustrated for Kids advertisements: A content analysis of prominent and supporting models. *Journal of Sports Management, 12*(1), 39-50.

Davis, T. (2004). The Secret Life Of Brands - Australian Children and their Brands: Implications for Advertisers. In P. Neijens, C. Hess, B. V. D. Putte & E. Smit (Eds.), *Content and Media Factors in Advertising.* Amsterdam: Het Spinhuis.

Fitzgerald, K. (2003). Newer leagues gird for grid action. *Advertising Age, 74*(43), S-2.

Gardyn, R. (2001). A League of Their Own. *American Demographics, 23*(3), 12-13.

Hite, C. F., & Hite, R. E. (1995). Reliance on brand by young children. *Journal of Marketing Research, 37,* 185-193.

Jackson, E. N. (2000). Sport Marketing (Book). *Journal of Sport Management, 14*(2), 188-190.

Jensen, J. (1996). Wayward sport leagues rediscover their youth. *Advertising Age, 67*(7), S2.

Jensen, J. (1998). NFL ad blitz targets next-generation fans. *Advertising Age, 69*(34), 8.

Ji, M. F. (2001). Children as potential relationship partners: A conceptual framework. In J. Myers & M. C. Gilly (Eds.), *Advances in Consumer Research* (Vol. 28). Salt Lake City: (forthcoming).

Kuzma, J. R., Veltri, F. R., Kuzma, A. T., & Miller, J. J. (2003). Negative Corporate Sponsor Information: The Impact on Consumer Attitudes and Purchase Intentions. *International Sports Journal, 7*(2), 140-147.

Levin, S. R., Petros, T. V., & Petrella, F. W. (1982). Preschoolers' awareness of television advertising. *Child Development, 53,* 933-937.

Macklin, M. C. (1996). Preschoolers' learning of brand names from visual cues. *Journal of Consumer Research, 23,* 251-258.

Martin, C. A., & Bush, A. J. (2000). Do role models influence teenagers' purchase intentions and behavior? *Journal of Consumer Marketing, 17*(5), 441-453.

Mravic, M., & Deitsch, R. (2003, 6/9/2003). Of a certain age. *Sports Illustrated, 98,* 23-26.

Oates, C., Blades, M., & Gunter, B. (2002). Children and television advertising: When do they understand persuasive intent? *Journal of Consumer Behavior, 1,* 238-245.

Pennington, B. (2004, 10/18/2004). Reading, writing and corporate sponsorship. *New York Times,* p. Op.

Pine, K. J., & Nash, A. (2003). Barbie or Betty? Preschool children's preferences for branded products and evidence for gender-linked differences. *Journal of Developmental and Behavioral Pediatrics, 24*(4), 219-224.

Pine, K. J., & Nash, A. (2005). *Dear Santa: The effects of television advertising on young children.* Unpublished manuscript, Hatfield, Herts, U.K.

Roedder John, D. (1999). Consumer socialization of children: A retrospective look at twenty-five years of research. *Journal of Consumer Research, 26,* 183-213.

Schooler, C., & Feighery, E. (1996). Seventh Graders' Self-Reported Exposure to Cigarette Marketing and its Relationship to Their Smoking Behavior. *American Journal of Public Health, 86*(9), 1216-1221.

Shugart, H. A. (2003). She shoots, she scores: Mediated constructions of contemporary female athletes in coverage of the 1999 US women's soccer team. *Western Journal of Communication, 67*(1), 1-31.

Slack, T. (1998). Studying the commercialization of Sport: the Need for Critical Analysis. *Sociology of Sport Online, 1*(1).

Steinberg, B., & Tkacik, M. (2003, 7/22). Should Brands Bryant Endorses Keep Him On? *Wall Street Journal,* p. B1.

Taveres, E. M., Rifas-Shiman, S. L., Field, A. E., Frazier, A. L., Colditz, G. A., & Gillman, M. W. (2004). The influence of wanting to look like media figures on adolescent physical activity. *Journal of Adolescent Health, 35*(1), 41-50.

Wenner, L. A. (1994). The Dream Team, Communicative Dirt, and the Marketing of Synergy: USA Basketball and Cross-Merchandising in Television Commercials. *Journal of Sport & Social Issues, 18*(1), 27-47.

INDEX

H

I

J

K

L

T